So You Want to
Be a Teacher?

So You Want to Be a Teacher?

What I Learned in Forty Years of Teaching

Katherine—
I love you.
Lib Brett

Elizabeth H. Brett
Teacher-by-Trade

Library of Congress Control Number:		2013907300
ISBN:	Hardcover	978-1-4836-2959-9
	Softcover	978-1-4836-2958-2
	Ebook	978-1-4836-2960-5

This book was printed in the United States of America.

Rev. date: 05/09/2013

To order additional copies of this book, contact:
Xlibris Corporation
1-888-795-4274
www.Xlibris.com
Orders@Xlibris.com
131019

CONTENTS

To my late husband, Ralph Brett

AN INTRODUCTION

My vocal cords, which received their first workout in the bedroom of a weathered dogtrot house on the banks of a Limestone County stream, would later bring sounds—some melodious, some discordant—to the ears of hundreds of students. My mother always said that my tongue would be a deciding factor in my life because I talked so early. When other youngsters were putting together phrases and ill-arranged word assortments, I was using whole sentences—some that attached themselves to each other with delightful clarity. Actually, what she said was "Your tongue will be your ruin," and from incidents I shall relate, one would think that she was clairvoyant. From a very early age, I loved books and conversations, so I suppose I have always had a love affair with words.

My mother said that somewhere in my genes existed an inclination that predetermined that I would be a teacher. From the time I was three, I tried to teach whatever objects I could collect that appeared to have the capacity to sit and absorb my teaching. My dolls were my first pupils. Later, pets that could be coerced to regiment themselves to a degree of civility became my unwilling class. I performed well under either condition: the docile manner of the dolls or the aggressive behavior of the animals. Misbehavior of the pets challenged me to talk louder or gesture more frequently in my efforts to share my "knowledge" with them. For a time, we lived near Ripley Elementary School, and I can remember being allowed on certain occasions to visit Mrs. Lucille's first-grade class where I sat in a wooden desk as she tenderly plied the pastoral minds of those a bit older than I. My parents had made me solemnly promise not to utter a word, but I could hardly obey because I was so enthralled with the atmosphere of school.

In May, my sixth birthday arrived, and I knew that come autumn, I would walk the halls of Athens Elementary School. I was so excited! The flag that flew above the school, the wide concrete walk that divided the grassy playground, the big outside water fountain with six faucets, the long flight of steps that led to the double doors—these were the harbingers of grandiose experiences that awaited me inside the school. How I loved the inside smell! Usually, there was a heady combination of smells—oiled wooden floors, bananas that protruded from the lunch sacks, and bouquets brought to the teacher from home flower gardens. How vividly I remember some scenes! My first-grade teacher drew a huge cherry tree on white poster and hung it on the side blackboard. Each limb had a pupil's name on it; a bright red dot representing a cherry appeared on the limb as a result of a good grade. How I worked to have a limb heavily laden!

At the end of that first exciting school year, I was placed in the third grade; therefore, as the years passed, whenever I felt depressed about my lack of accomplishments, I could always say to myself, "Well, at least I skipped the second grade!" How blessed I was always to have had excellent elementary-school teachers. It is vitally important that students are given a firm foundation—a solid base for later educational challenges. In the fifth grade, my teacher inspired me to climb the highest rung of the learning ladder by her stern standards of discipline. As much as I loved to hear the sound of my own voice, I absolutely refrained from talking in class because her cure for such a transgression was to force a tablespoon of castor oil into one's mouth and instantly clap tape over the mouth (tape not subject to removal). Can you believe that she was married to a minister of the Gospel? At times, I pictured her in medieval days as a consultant for the Holy Inquisition as it used methods of torture to eradicate heresy.

My teacher in the sixth grade was a superb teacher who was also a strict disciplinarian. How well I remember the shame and humiliation everyone felt for the lad whose request to go to the restroom was refused and who then created a puddle on the floor beneath his desk. How well I remember her taking from another hapless sixth-grade boy a Three Musketeers candy bar, which he was about to unwrap and consume stealthily. She unwrapped and ate it with gusto in front of the entire class. Back in those school days, when the teacher left the room (a very infrequent occurrence), she left a student standing at the front blackboard "taking names" of those who misbehaved. What an unfair practice!

That year in our room was a lanky red-haired troublemaker who always misbehaved and usually blamed someone else. His name is permanently engraved upon my brain, but I shall not reveal it. That particular day, the teacher left me with the responsibility of maintaining order. I was somewhat apprehensive lest this class bully with the red hair decide to hone his skills of intimidation; my fears were well-founded. Immediately, the bully began taunting some of the less-aggressive pupils. He then bragged to me that I had better not put his name on the blackboard as I would suffer the consequences of his displeasure at such an act. A fault of mine, which through the years has sometimes cost me dearly, is that I do not "suffer fools gladly." I wheeled around, and with bold I-am-not-afraid-of-you strokes, I wrote his name, whereupon he threw an eraser at me with great velocity and accuracy. It struck me in the head; blood began to gush from my long brown tresses. Erasers in those days had very hard backs and, when thrown with speed, could be dangerous weapons. The teacher returned, my wound was attended to, the missile dispatcher was punished, and my parents were placated. My mother had endured an encounter with a bully when she was in the sixth grade, but she had reacted with much more true grit than I did. When her bully grabbed her toboggan off her head as a group walked home from school on a cold winter's day, she ran after him, caught him, threw him down, and beat his head against the frozen ground. I am sure her memory of that incident helped her to accept my situation; at least, my bully was punished in a more humane fashion.

As I grew up in Athens, the school system was divided on three levels—elementary, junior high, and high school. I recall with great pleasure those happy days. I loved each of my teachers: from the music teacher (whose husband was in the air force and who had us end each concert with a rousing rendition of "Off We Go into the Wild Blue Yonder") to the spirited spinster who valiantly struggled to instill in us a knowledge of and appreciation for mathematics.

Though I do not yearn to return to 1943-47, class reunions provide sentimental journeys of wonderful times. Most of the high school teachers were special, but for the first time, I encountered and endured two or three who would be perfect examples for a chapter entitled "Imperfect Teaching Techniques." Through all of my education including my college days, I never wavered from my choice of teaching as a career. Subconsciously, I believe I really wanted to be an actress, and teaching gave me a captive audience!

CHAPTER ONE

Students: The Pleasure of Their Company

Forty years of daily contact with students, excluding holidays and summers, made me a better occupant of this orb that we call Earth because I learned so much from them. *Love* is a powerful four-letter word; and with few exceptions, I loved my students—the outstanding, the obnoxious, and the otherwise. Some of these students became scholars who diligently applied their minds to acquiring knowledge in many areas, some were dilettantes who dabbled in learning as a pastime, and some simply occupied seats in the classroom.

May I share with you some lessons I learned from my students?

1. The first lesson I learned from my students was to be slow to criticize.

When I took up my first essay assignments, I exercised little or no restraint in marking them; my red pen had a vigorous workout. The returned papers, which looked as though they needed blood transfusions, were received with looks of dismay and disappointment while I surveyed my grammatical domain, confident that I had taught a good lesson in exposing their grammatical ineptness. Whose fault was it that they were so inept? Quickly, I learned to accentuate the positive. A veteran teacher told me always to look (modern grammar allows for split infinitives, as I am told, but I am absolutely too old to embrace such a transgression!) for something to compliment; pats on the back are usually very appreciated if they are deserved, so I learned to wrap constructive criticism in layers of praise—like an Oreo cookie (praise, criticism, praise).

Once, a student baffled me completely when she called me at home with a question. In teaching grammar, I often used the board; after all, chalk dust is part of the process. I was teaching the difference between transitive active and transitive passive verbs, so I turned and boldly wrote on the board TA-DO—a *transitive active*

13

verb has to have a *direct object*. About a week later, I assigned a test on the material we had just covered. The phone rang, and I heard the sweet voice of one of my really shy female students say, "Mrs. Brett, will you please tell me what a *tado* is?" She had written my abbreviation as one word and had pronounced it that way as well. How easily I could have been overly critical of her lack of attention and concentration.

Many years ago, I experienced headaches so severe that I sought medical help. After all kinds of tests and no solution, I was told by someone who had felt the same pain that she felt much better after visiting a local chiropractor, so I decided to give that procedure a try. Now, may I retrace my steps? The chiropractor whom I called had been one of my students at Athens High School. He was an excellent student and a nice lad; however, as my students were wont to do, one day, he felt compelled to accentuate my class with some antics of his own. World War I was the topic of study, and I had just told the class that William McAdoo served as Woodrow Wilson's director general of United States railroads from 1917 until 1919 while the government operated them as a wartime measure. Looking toward the back of the room, I saw a student strumming an imaginary guitar and silently mouthing "McAdoo-McAdoo-McAdoo." Irritated that my lecture had such an entertaining effect on him, I told him to go to the front of the class and let them see what he was doing as I was lecturing. He pleaded not to come, but I was the teacher—the symbol of absolute authority. I insisted, and he came to the front of the class where he strummed and mouthed, much to the delight of his comrades.

Now back to my headaches. I called this student who had become a chiropractor, made an appointment, went to his clinic, removed my garments, put on a little robe, and lay on the adjustment couch. He leaned over and whispered, "McAdoo-McAdoo-McAdoo!" I figured that I was at his mercy.

In a Humanities class one year, there was a student who certainly qualified as a scholar because the only exercise he enjoyed was one of the mental types. He paid no attention to his body's physical needs, but he kept his mind alert by reading about every subject. The written words sustained him. He was therefore very knowledgeable; he qualified as a nerd long before we knew the word. Because he knew so much about almost everything, he had perfected the practice of condescension to a fine degree. He exhibited an air of superiority by making remarks under his breath or giving withering looks when another student answered a question incorrectly. I tried to chide him gently out of his rudeness into the realm of acceptable behavior, but frequently, his baser instincts overcame my correcting tactics. Such a time coincided with my already having a bad day at school; my biorhythms must have been out of balance, so when the head varsity cheerleader gave a wrong answer and he guffawed, my last drop of mercy toward him evaporated. I demanded that he go to the front of the room and lead a cheer, using appropriate motions and acrobatics. What a dismal failure he was as a cheerleader! How the class enjoyed his feeble efforts and his embarrassment! How ashamed I should have been for resorting to such Machiavellian techniques! Was a valuable lesson taught here? Was a valuable lesson learned here?

When I taught literature and history, I often required students to memorize poetry such as "Thanatopsis" or beautiful passages from history such as the Gettysburg Address. Thoughts like these committed to memory have often sustained people in times of turmoil or stress; I wanted nourishing thoughts to occupy the minds of my students forever. When I assigned memory work, there were always some students who viewed such an assignment as a waste of time, so they looked for some way to avoid the memory work. One way was to write the assigned passage or poem prior to coming to class and then slip that paper into the stack of legitimate papers as they were being collected. One day, I told the class to count down five whole lines on the sheet of paper and to begin writing their memory work on the sixth line; I had heard via the school rumor mill about a certain student's boasting about how he always cheated on his memory work, so I thought my new plan might at least challenge him. In a short while, this student handed in his prewritten memory work, which began on the first whole line. When I pointed out this error, he said he did not hear my instructions about beginning on the sixth line. When everyone had finished, I told Mr. Fail-to-Memorize to come to the front of the room and recite the passage. Looking a bit askance, he came, opened his mouth, and vomited everywhere. Two of us learned valuable lessons that day.

2.　The second lesson I learned from my students was that some students can easily be led, but others require a bit of a push.

Have you ever observed a flock of geese flying in perfect formation against an autumn sky? Sometimes a goose will lead; at other times, that same goose may honk from behind. I learned that I could not always be the head goose—sometimes I had to be a honker and encourage from behind.

Once, I participated in an innovative educational technique called team teaching wherein two teachers taught in a class together—for example, American literature and American history interwoven. My partner was a young man who was an assistant football coach; he was a joy as a partner because he and I shared the same work ethic. Both of us believed that discipline must prevail for learning to occur. There were a few graceful gliders on the Lake of Learning in class, but most of them were painful plodders interested in punk music and horror movies. What a challenge! It was very difficult to motivate this group to enjoy the poetry of Longfellow or the diplomacy of Thomas Jefferson; perhaps we could have expressed the beautifully stated ideas of those giants in a form the students would have recognized and appreciated, but we refused to dilute the material. We were not permitted to discipline any student; for any transgression, a student had to be sent to the principal's office where only he had the authority to write the student's name in a book. Wasn't that strange? Only the principal's handwriting appeared in that book.

One day, a girl who was usually noncooperative in a placid sort of way became downright obnoxious when she realized how little she knew about the topic under discussion. When I gently chastised her for her attitude, she scowled at me, snatched a piece from her notebook, scribbled something on it, and "accidently" dropped it on the floor. When the class was over and she had not retrieved the crumpled paper, I picked it up. Would you believe that on it she had written, "Go to hell, Mrs. Brett!"? In righteous indignation (we teachers travel frequently in the phrase, don't we?), I marched to the principal's office with the offensive paper clutched in my hand. My anger overcame my obedience to the principal's edict that only he could write in the "sin" book. I turned it toward me on the counter, opened it to the proper date, and proclaimed in black ink the name of the student and her conduct. What was the consequence of my conduct? She received an admonition about directing a teacher to an undesirable locale, and I received a reprimand for daring to write in the sacred book.

Once a year, a troubled young man roamed the halls of Athens High School. I am sure that there were others equally as troubled, but I knew of this one only. The first time I saw him, I was walking down the hall when I heard a loud voice from another teacher's room. Stepping to her open door, I realized that she was not in the room and that most of the students were gathered in a circle as they encouraged two students who were about to engage in fisticuffs. I entered the room and was unsuccessfully trying to break up the fight when an athlete who was passing by came to my aid. He and I escorted the two combatants to the principal's office, and I thought my part in this episode was over. The principal later came to my room to see if he could place the troubled teenager who instigated this incident in one of my Humanities classes; I agreed, but the teenager did not. He informed the principal in "erudite" street language that he would terminate his educational career before he would be in my class because "she is the work of the devil." I never knew the source of his knowledge regarding my spiritual affiliations, but he was not placed in my class. From that time on, whenever I saw him in the hallways, I would speak to him in a pleasant manner and call him by name, but a grumpy "harrumph" was the only acknowledgment I ever received from him.

3.   The third lesson I learned from my students was to recognize the power of motivation and to search for the path that would stimulate their brain cells.

Once, I lost thirty pounds because I wanted to be slimmer than my husband's high school sweetheart when we attended his twenty-fifth class reunion. That meeting with her was a powerful motivating factor for me! In a section of *Reader's Digest* entitled "Personal Glimpses," Nona Louise Dunbar had the following item that I deem an excellent example of motivation:

Our athlete, Mohammed Ali remembered a once-in-a-lifetime bicycle which his parents gave him when he was a kid. Proud and happy, he parked it outside a gym one day, and somebody stole it. It broke his heart. He told a policeman about the theft and also told him that he was going to find the guy who stole his bicycle and beat him up. When the policeman discovered that Ali did not know how to fight, he offered to teach him. That is how he got into boxing. He never found the thief, but every time he was in the ring, he pretended his opponent was the guy who stole his bicycle.

For many years, Ralph, my husband, was an elementary school principal. One year, the fourth-grade boys were unusually unruly, especially in the restroom. Good ideas often come from ordinary situations, and a grand idea occurred to my husband when he learned that the high school Athletic Department was about to purchase a new camera to film the football games. He requested and received the old camera, which he had his maintenance men install in the restroom used by the fourth-grade boys. Only he and these men and the teachers knew that the camera was not connected; it just appeared to be. Behavior improved, and the problem appeared to be solved; however, one boy who was apparently more adventuresome than his buddies decided to test the authenticity of the device. He gave the camera "the finger." Nothing happened as a result of his action, so he felt constrained to brag about his restroom rebellion, even to the teacher.

"That camera that Mr. Brett put in the restroom doesn't work. I gave it 'the finger,' and I was never called to the office."

The quick-thinking teacher inquired, "When did you do this?"

"Day before yesterday."

"Well, Mr. Brett looks at the film only on Friday." Then the teacher immediately informed my husband of the situation.

On Friday, my husband called the student to the office and disciplined him. Such cooperation between principal and teacher makes a good team.

That same year, a second-grade boy passed a note to a second-grade girl. Now, passing notes between would-be sweethearts is just indicative of first-love activities on a school level, but this particular signed note earned an *R* rating. "I want to F—you," the note announced. The little girl gave this startling bit of news to her teacher who promptly took the boy and note to my husband's office.

After looking at the note, my husband ordered the second-grade boy to read it to him. The child read, "I want to—" and stopped. When told to continue reading, he insisted that he did not know the next word.

"Well, you wrote it. You certainly must know what it is," my husband said.

"No, sir. I just put some letters down, and this is the word they made." Creativity and vulgarity—what a combination!

Teachers want all the acorns to become oaks, but sometimes an intellectual drought will occur. One year, there were three athletes in one of my classes who seemed determined to ignore my teaching as well as the common courtesies usually required by teachers, such as not chewing gum, not slumping in the seat, and not removing shoes. One lad seemed to have a real aversion to wearing shoes. Repeatedly, I asked him not to take his shoes off, and for a time, he cooperated; however, one day during an exam, as he was absorbed in thought, he slipped off his loafers and "toed" them out in the aisle. As was my custom, I tried to encourage and maintain class honesty by patrolling the aisles. Suddenly I saw them—offensive objects that they were. Very quietly, I picked them up and dropped them out of the first-floor window. Obviously, I was not observed because no one said anything. When the class was over, the lad began to look for his shoes. Finally, I told him what I had done and why I had done it. He looked out the window, turned to me, and announced that the shoes were gone. At first, I did not believe him, so I went to the window myself. No shoes! They were gone! Both shoes were gone! I had, at the moment, a mounting curiosity to know what happened to those loafers, and I also had an irate student who would violate a school rule by going to his next class sans shoes. I had to go to the principal and inform him of my latest misdeed, all the while disguising my fault in the episode as an attempt to teach the student a lesson. The news traveled fast around the school. Students absolutely love incidents in which they are the victims and teachers are the miscreants. Would you believe that later that afternoon someone walking on Beaty Street found both of those shoes, not at all damaged and lying close together? The favorite theory was that dogs took them. We never knew.

The first year I taught, I was assigned a group of seventh graders for homeroom and language arts. One young man, now deceased, was the class clown—not mean, just mischievous. He informed me that during all his previous school days, he had behaved that way, and he did not plan to change. He lived up to this declaration as well as to his reputation. The teachers were allowed to paddle students who had earned such punishment, so I took him out in the hall when he next misbehaved, and I whacked him three times—three resounding blows that could readily be heard in the classroom. I felt it necessary to give him as hard a lick each time as I could muster because he had bragged earlier that no teacher had ever made him cry. Now how could I resist this gauntlet flung so carelessly upon the oiled floor? His blue eyes filled with tears, and then he began to sob. This reaction to the paddling was probably from humiliation rather than damage to his posterior. He sobbed and sobbed until, throwing future disciplinary actions to the wind, I comforted him and told him I would buy him a Popsicle at afternoon recess if he would hush. Finally, his sobs subsided. The class clown soon became an attentive, well-behaved young man whom I adored. I was not aware that he had labeled me "the meanest woman God ever made." Later, I learned of this honor he had granted me.

4. The fourth lesson I learned from my students was to appreciate the students for who they were as well as what they could become.

Brash students caused me to look beneath the surface and to heed the unspoken pleas for reassurance. Probably, only educators realize how many budget crunches our profession has endured. Once, at Athens High School, the principal instructed the faculty that no supplies were to be ordered; no money was to be spent without his approval. We were reminded that such approval was highly unlikely to be forthcoming. For several years, I had ordered the film *Medea* with Judith Anderson; she was such a powerful actress, and the story was so beautifully presented that I deemed this a worthwhile teaching tool. This particular year, I did not even ask to order the film because it was so expensive that I knew I would not receive approval. Can you imagine my amazement when I was called to the principal's office to view, lying on his desk, the film *Medea* addressed to me at the high school? Immediately, I began to deny my disobedience. Triumphantly (principals do like to triumph!), he produced the order blank, and there in my handwriting was the evidence. He was indignant, to say the least. I was baffled, to say the least. I never really convinced him that I was innocent, so I determined that I would call upon my very own Renegade Roster to get to the bottom of the mystery, and they did!

There was a previous employed person at the school as aide of all activities. Though physically impaired and in a wheelchair, intellectually, he was in the top ranks. He had a pet squirrel, which he kept at the school. Once, I had befriended him by alerting him to a squirrel search, which the principal was about to instigate, and he repaid me by forging my signature and ordering the film. When I confronted him, he said, "You have always liked that film, and I wanted you to have it." I suppose he thought, once the film had arrived, the principal would bestow his approval. We stood together for our punishment—a teacher desiring a teaching tool and a worker hiding a woodland creature.

One year, a student of mine at Athens High School became a fixture in the principal's office because of his mischievous manner. He was not a bad boy; he simply saw life as a lesson in levity. His affectionate attitude toward me was probably the reason that I never sent him to the principal's office; also, I prided myself on handling my own discipline. One day when we were on a different class schedule, I sent him to the office with a question about procedure; before he could ask the question, the principal snatched him up and paddled him (yes, in those days of yore, the principal could paddle without a witness). That action was an affront to both the student's dignity and my reputation for handling my own problems. Needless to say, my mother's admonition that my tongue would be my ruin nearly proved true that day. The principal and I engaged in a very serious dialogue.

One year when six boys who I thought should have been inducted into the National Honor Society were not inducted because of infractions in the classroom, my mouth almost proved to be a stumbling block to me again. Their pretenses at not being disappointed were so transparent that a person with her head totally in the sand would have known. My argument on their behalf was that they should have been written up and sent to the principal's office if their behavior had been offensive enough to warrant no consideration for the Honor Society. As I have said before, I believe that teachers should be as responsible as they possibly can for the discipline in their classrooms, but if behavior is disruptive and attempts to correct it are not heeded, a higher power needs to be notified. (Isn't a higher power a good synonym for a principal?) The day after the National Honor Society induction, these six boys (all seniors) showed up at school wearing yellow shirts that boldly proclaimed SOCIETY OF THUGS. They brought me a yellow shirt that arrogantly announced in letters on the front: SPONSOR OF SOCIETY OF THUGS. (I understand this incident occurred again after I left the high school with another teacher who showed sympathy for the plight of these students.)
Quickly, the students were summoned to the office and sent home to change shirts. How I wish I could relate a different ending to this story, but truth must prevail. As I learned of their punishment, my mean genes took control of my body, and I went to the restroom where I exchanged my schoolmarm blouse for the gaudy gift my beloved renegades had bestowed upon me. I do not have to tell you that my ill-tempered victory was short-lived. The military retiree (one of my favorite principals), who prided himself on running a tight ship, in angry tones gave me the option of putting my blouse on or going home. When I complied with his request, I felt I truly had experienced a hollow victory. I showed my support to those I loved, but oh, it was a brief burst of belligerence!

One Halloween in a small Alabama town, the students' creative juices flowed amok. Some of the students who felt animosity toward a certain teacher painted her front porch completely with molasses and white chicken feathers. I shudder to think how many naked fowls greeted November that year! Three bicycles were found tied to the tops of telephone poles, but the crowning achievement occurred at the high school. When the principal unlocked the doors the morning after Halloween, he beheld an unusual sight. A large farm wagon rested in the front hall of the school. There was barely room for one person to squeeze by on either side. A perplexed principal stood first at the front of the wagon and then at the back of the wagon, his brow furrowed as he tried to figure out how the Halloween Houdini Hoodlums had gotten the wagon through the doors of the school. As the day went on, the students became so proud of this deed that their arrogance prodded them into claiming credit. They were delighted to explain how they had disassembled the vehicle, only to reassemble it inside the building. They were charged with breaking and entering, but the next issue of the school newspaper proclaimed their creativity (and hard labor!) in bold headlines.

For years, I taught a course entitled Humanities at Athens High School. The class syllabus encompassed art, theology, literature, history, and philosophy—a general background centered in great ideas and enhanced by lessons in civility and gentility. Early each spring, the Humanities classes produced a pageant; the students did all the work, stage decorations, and the performances that included songs, dances, and skits. I always passed around a sheet that each student signed to indicate what he or she wished to do in the pageant. One student wrote, "Mrs. Brett, I shall do anything you want me to except pose in the nude!"

We usually raised a sizeable sum of money that I used to take the students (about eighty each year) on a long weekend educational trip. We had to use two buses to transport the students. Another teacher rode one bus, and I rode the other. I knew each student well and trusted each one, yet I felt so accountable for their well-being and so anxious that they not completely pull the wool over my eyes that she and I slept very little the two or three nights we were gone.

Once, we went to Callaway Gardens, from whence we could visit Warm Springs, Georgia, and see where FDR (whom we had studied) died. The students were settled in cabins in the woods adjoining the area of the main lodge. I had told the students that they had to be in their assigned cabins by midnight and not to venture out again. There was a refreshment pavilion approximately in the center of the cabins we were occupying. The other teacher and I were sitting with our backs to the trunk of a large tree when, about 1:00 a.m., we heard a door open and close. Silently, we moved toward the path leading to the refreshment pavilion. In a moment, here came a hefty football hero, strutting along, whistling softly. When he reached our hiding place behind a bush, I stepped out and said, "Where are you going?" He accused me of trying to make him have a heart attack. I accused him of civil disobedience!

5. The fifth lesson I learned from my students was to accept the awesome challenge of lost causes—students who came to my classes in a damaged state and in dire need of tender, loving care. Even though I tried valiantly to rescue these wayward ones, I did not always succeed.

Near the end of my career at Athens High School, the principal requested and received permission from the State Department of Education for us to begin a two-hour afternoon class (1:00-3:00) called Special Instructional Services. I was the teacher, and after a couple of weeks, I determined that a more appropriate name for the class could have been "In the Belly of the Whale." The principal selected from grades 9 to 12—male and female, black and white—the sixteen students who had been the worst troublemakers the first semester. We convened in the band room because it was relatively isolated. Though I first equated my position to that of a lion tamer, I grew very fond of these sixteen mortals. The first week, I asked the students to write on a paper I passed around something or someone that or who would interest them. One student wrote "Daryl Dawkins" (a person with whom I did not even have a passing acquaintance). I began to research and discovered information about him that would lead me down avenues whereby I might teach civility and gentility. The second person listed was Cassius Clay, who led me to teach about the Vietnam conflict. By meeting these students on common ground, by the second six weeks, I was teaching a modified version of the Humanities curriculum.

One of the young white males used, as a part of his vocabulary, that odious phrase *motherf—*; he never abbreviated it. I tried a positive attitude toward him. I exercised unending patience with him, but he continued to use this terminology. I suppose I would be arrested nowadays for what I did next to try to solve this problem. One day, when all my horoscope signs were obviously wrong and I had endured a trying day, I heard him call someone in SIS by his favorite vulgar label. I marched over to him, grabbed him by the collar, and right in his face, I said, "If you ever say motherf—again in my hearing, I am going to do my best to slap the hell out of you." I used no abbreviations. The class appeared absolutely shell shocked to hear these street words being used in the band room by a member of the faculty. As the obscenities speaker did not respond to my actions, I asked, "Do you understand me?" Meekly, he replied in the affirmative; I had finally broken his language barrier. Would you believe he went all the way to the last two weeks of school without slipping a single time?

All the other classes were going on field trips, so naturally, this unique group wanted to go on a field trip. I pleaded with the principal, and hesitantly, he agreed we could go on a short trip on a school bus driven by a male faculty member. As we boarded the bus in front of the high school, another class member tripped my vulgar-vocabulary person, and he shouted, "I'll get you later, you motherf—!" Again I pleaded, and we were permitted to go on the trip because this young man had indeed made progress.

During the following summer, this student rang our doorbell in the middle of the night. He was bloody and bruised. Between bouts of sobbing, he related to us how his father had physically abused him for years. That particular night, his father had tied him to a tree with a heavy rope and then had beaten him. He admonished my husband and me again and again that we must not tell anyone. Henry David Thoreau said, "Most men live lives of quiet desperation." How often I wondered how many students live lives of quiet desperation.

Occasionally, the class was interrupted by the local police who needed to question one of my charges. One young man was called out of my class one afternoon to be questioned about a shoplifting episode at a discount store in Athens called Ashley's. When he came back into the room, he indignantly announced in a voice loud enough to be heard all over the room, "Mrs. Brett, they tried to accuse me of shoplifting at Ashley's. You know I wouldn't wear anything that came from that store!"

Because I loved quotes on every subject, I wished to arouse in each of my students this same appreciation, so every day when they entered my room, they saw a quote on the board followed by its source. They were expected to memorize the quote and the source, be able to paraphrase it, and be able to give its significance. One autumn night, about ten o'clock, my phone rang. When I answered, one of my eleventh-grade Humanities students announced, "Mrs. Brett, we have been to the Country Club [an Ardmore, Tennessee, beer joint frequented by the students], and—has had too much to drink. He is throwing up so much that he probably won't be able to come to school tomorrow. We thought you might like to know." This overindulgent student was actually an outstanding scholar as well as a promising athlete. I assured the talebearers that when next I encountered—, I would let him know that I had been informed of his infirmity. Pondering the incident, I finally came to the conclusion that I would use the next day's quote to let—know that his drinking buddies had ratted on him. On the board, I wrote, "Bacchus has drowned more men than Neptune" (Anonymous).

He did come to school. He took one look at the board and then said to me, "Who told you?"

Once, a teacher, young and inexperienced, who wanted to ingratiate himself with the high schoolers, shared details of his personal life with them. His room was next to mine; therefore, I often felt a real need to help him with his discipline. (Believe it or not, I controlled this feeling and did not interfere.) When my class was doing written work and I was not talking, we could hear what was occurring in his room. One winter day, he came to school with the news that his wife was pregnant. After telling the teachers the happy news, he decided he would tell his students. When his first class convened, he chose to tell him in this manner: "Soon at our house, we shall hear the patter of little feet."

Immediately, a student shouted, "Are you going to buy a dog?"

6.   The sixth lesson I learned from my students was to realize the importance of creating a wee bit of magic in the classroom every now and then.

Once, in a high school history class, I opened a textbook that was lying on the floor, whereupon I discovered the following notation in the front: "In case of a flood, stand on this. It is dry as dirt." Did this ever challenge me to create a little magic? I looked at the problem as an opportunity to exercise my brain cells and initiate some thought-provoking discussions. I began to invite area people who could enlighten my students—World War II veterans, recent travelers to Russia and to China, an international debutante prior to World War II, etc. The possibilities were limitless.

Students always loved to study about wars. In American history, I truly enjoyed teaching about World War I and World War II because so many resources were available. The students enjoyed studying about Alvin C. York, a highly decorated soldier of WWI; I suppose the fact that he grew up in Tennessee just a bit north of us made him even more interesting. One night, a carload of the eleventh graders who had recently studied York's biography had gone to Tennessee to partake of their favorite brew. On the way home, they were stopped by a constable for speeding. Thank goodness, they were not totally inebriated, just happy. One of them noticed that the last name on the constable's identification tag was York, so this alert drinker inquired if the constable knew Alvin C. York. He replied that Alvin C. York, then deceased, was his uncle. The students then began to regale this keeper of the law with information about his uncle; how delighted they were when he gave them a warning and sent them on their way. They could hardly wait to tell me how their knowledge of history had served a purpose! They had experienced a reason to study the past.

Creativity is a welcome trait of aspiring writers. I have kept an essay written by one of my English students to complete an assignment on the topic "Circumstances Are Not Always What They Seem." I shall paraphrase this student's literary effort:

"On a first date, a young man was driving his girl down a country lane. She was fashionably attired in a white blouse and a red-and-white skirt accentuated by a row of pearl buttons all down the front. As they enjoyed a lively conversation, the boy kept looking at her skirt. As he continued to focus his attention on her lower regions, she began to be concerned that he was a rapist; her suspicions were almost confirmed when he pulled off on a side road, grabbed her, and began to snatch the buttons off her skirt. You see, this lad was a button collector!"

I always wondered what thoughts lurked beneath the surface of that student's mind.

The year Athens High School and the all-black Trinity High School integrated was one learning experience after another for me. I felt such compassion for those students who were forced to leave a school rich in tradition and steeped in their culture to attend a school completely alien to them. We managed to smooth the rough spots and learned to respect and appreciate one another. How I grew to love some of those wonderful young people!

There was a young man starved for the secrets of the written word who would immediately seek more information on someone or something mentioned in class. There was a precious sophomore girl who, at first, was so sure that I would not be fair in my grading system that she carefully scrutinized each of her returned papers and then compared the grade with that of a white student. There was a promising athlete who struggled with academics so he could be an asset to the school on Friday football nights. One young man so academically gifted joined the army when he graduated; he wrote to me from his base in Germany and told me of historic sites in Europe he had visited during his free time. I had not realized that our study of these places had so impressed him that he wished to visit them. My favorite correspondence from him, which rests safely with items I cherish most, was a note that stated, "If I could have had a white mother along with my own sweet mother, I would have chosen you."

Teaching brought in meager money, but ah, the other rewards! Some of my Trinity students were wonderfully adept at inserting their beliefs and comments into classroom activities. One day, I was summoned to the office. While I was gone, one of the black students decided to preach a sermon. I have no doubt that the class (as well as I) needed to hear it, but the time and place were improper. Just as I rounded the corner and was returning to my room, I heard him say, "I am the Resurrection and the Life."

The integrated group was sitting quietly; they were probably fascinated by the eloquence of this delivery. Sweeping into the room, I announced, "You will need resurrecting if you don't sit down and hush."

With that smart remark, I resumed control of my classroom. This young man proved to be an excellent student, especially when we studied the Hebrews.

While teaching in a high school in a small Alabama town, Ralph and I learned to love the septuagenarian who used her aged voice to teach music and her shaky limbs to conduct the choir. But alas! She was an excellent recruit for drivers' school. With reckless abandon, she drove an ancient Chevrolet and always parked outside the windows of the room where I taught English. One day, as I was attempting to explain what constituted a dangling participle to a group who were woefully inadequate in their perception of participles, I happened to look out the window. What I beheld amazed me!

"Get away from the wall!" I shouted to the students occupying that row of seats. They managed to exit that portion of the room just before Miss—hit it full force. The wall crumbled and the windows shattered, and the car became the car used in the fall festival to raise money (you know, the event where, for a fee, a person is allowed to hit a vehicle with a sledgehammer). Miss—was all right, just a bit more dazed than usual. We never really knew what happened.

7.   The seventh lesson I learned from my students was to be willing to share my time outside of school with the students. Outside-of-school time is quality student time. I enjoyed charming conversations from normally silent shy students as we sat in my den.

Sometimes, groups of students who needed extra review before a major exam would convene at my house. At times, the Humanities classes would meet at the high school library at night to watch a classic movie and discuss it. My home phone number was always available.

One does not teach forty years without experiencing tragedy in the lives of the students and in the community. Henry Wadsworth Longfellow wrote, "Into each life some rain must fall." How true! There were times when I felt we had endured a deluge. Death masquerading as speeding autos claimed several of our youth. The camaraderie that existed between teachers and students helped us to prevail through these tough times. How poignantly I recall a young man who was killed in a car wreck a week before graduation; his mother requested that a school official place his diploma in the open casket. His friend and fellow students sang "How Great Thou Art," and many handkerchiefs were dampened. How well I remember the beautiful junior on her way to feed her horses when she was killed in a road accident. Her mother placed a favorite stuffed animal in the casket at the service, and sobs were heard from macho individuals as well as from those more inclined to emotional outbursts. With a pain in my heart, I think of a highly intelligent tenth grader who failed to return home at his appointed time one night. The next morning, his body was found; the car in which he and three other boys were riding had not negotiated a fearsome curve, and all but one had died. The following week, his sister (who was in middle school) showed up in his seat in my classroom. The two principals—middle school and high school—left the situation alone; and after four days, she returned to her regular class schedule.

Then there were lesser tragedies involving needs. We were accustomed to filling Thanksgiving and Christmas baskets for the needy. Families by number rather than by name were assigned to each homeroom or club that wished to participate. My students always participated very generously. In one of my classes, a lad came to my desk and privately inquired about getting a Thanksgiving basket for his needy but proud family. I shall always remember with love and gratitude how the faculty responded to this request and what joy we experienced at his reaction. It was too late when we received his entreaty to go through proper channels, but the mission was accomplished anyway.

William Faulkner said, "Man shall not merely endure; he shall prevail." Time spent outside of school helped the students to establish a relationship with me that enabled us to overcome adversities.

Humanities was an elective class, so usually, students who did not wish to meet my requirements did not sign up for the class. Once in a while, the principal would put a student who was having difficulty in another class in Humanities; these recruits sometimes presented a real challenge. One young man whose idea of a classic was a comic book forced me to discover that the classics were available in comic books, so with him, I operated on the premise that reading good literature in any form was preferable to not reading at all. One day as we were reviewing for a major examination, I had a huge assortment of Tootsie Pops; a correct answer garnered a Tootsie Pop. Some of the students were amassing mounds of these tasty morsels. My method of operation as I asked the questions was to move about the room so that I could observe any extracurricular activity that might prove to be disadvantageous to the students' academic welfare. As I passed this young man's seat, I heard him mutter, "Ain't no way I'm gonna get one of them suckers." This remark gave me cause for reflection; was I enhancing his sense of inferiority by pointing out the obvious—not with words but with Tootsie Pops?

This same student exhibited the greatest degree of sensitivity when we studied the Holocaust. I had purchased large glossy pictures of the concentration camps in Germany during World War II—pictures taken by the liberating armies. As he looked at these reminders of "man's inhumanity toward man," he said over and over, "Those poor people." At the end of the class, he asked if he might take the pictures home to show his mother. This lad taught all of us something we did not get from books.

8.   The eighth lesson I learned from my students was to be honest with them, absolutely and completely.

Most students have no conception of hypocrisy; it is a word they could not fit into a crossword puzzle. From the high school sophomore who remarked that I had worn the same outfit two times in one week to the second grader in Athens

Elementary School who inquired of a gray-hair substitute if she were the oldest woman God ever made—students are refreshingly candid. They expect no less from teachers. What happiness it gave some of my students to hear me say, "I don't know."

Frequently, students in the field of education at the local college visited classes at the high school as a prelude to a college course entitled "Practice Teaching." I never minded having these people in my room; I simply ignored them as they needed to observe a teacher teaching as she normally taught. One day, I needed to have been more thoughtful; isn't it amazing what we can learn about ourselves in retrospect? We were studying connotation and denotation. In the front seat on the second row sat a true son of the South steeped in Southern tradition and totally devoted to Ole Miss. He loved the confederacy and believed that "the South could have whipped the Yankees with hickory sticks had they agreed to fight with them." When I asked for an example of connotation, he raised his hand and answered, "Damn Yankee." I never once considered that perhaps in the college group, there were some souls from north of the Mason-Dixon Line, so I complimented him on his apt reply. A couple of days later, I was called to the principal's office and informed that I had been discussed in the college class and the remarks had not been complimentary. Those visitors to my class who believed that the political persuasions and economics beliefs of their ancestors had justified the unpleasantness between the North and the South felt they had been castigated. I was told to be more considerate in my classroom.

Sometimes, we teachers make slips of the tongue. Once, a high school English instructor at Athens High School assigned a term paper to her eleventh-grade class early in the year. She allowed the students to choose their topics, subject to her approval. One lanky lad chose "The Effects of Venereal Disease upon Today's Society." A few days later, as she was returning from her lunch break, she saw several young men lounging near the library door. Approaching one, she inquired, "Son, how are you coming with your venereal disease?" It was not the student she thought; this young man did not know her. He was very embarrassed; he came to my office to ask of me, "What is wrong with that woman?" Needless to say, he was the source of amusement for some students for quite a while.

Some students love to cheat. Sometimes they spend far more time on ways to put one over on the teacher than would be required for them to learn their lessons. Once, I taught one year at a school where the concept of team teaching was introduced. Twin boys whom their mother would not permit to be separated (even by seats) were notorious cheaters. They outwitted me for quite some time, but one day, the one who sat behind the other totally confirmed my suspicions. On a history test to a fill-in-the-blank, the student in the first seat wrote, "I don't know." His brother—seated right behind him—wrote, "I don't either."

One young man whose career objective was engineering really had me going for a time. He never knew much in class, but he always did well on tests. No wonder! He had removed the inside of his watch, and for each test, he inserted a new scroll that he moved by winding his watch. Think of the time he spent before each test, preparing the cheat scroll. What I learned from this was to give essay questions that required some knowledge and a sense of organization.

Once, when I was totally exhausted from grading so many essays and term papers and book reviews, I took a job as a high school counselor. I loved the students, the faculty, and the administration, but quickly I realized that I was in the wrong genre. Oh, how I missed teaching! While I was there, the state mandated that achievement tests be administered on all levels. This task fell to me. High school and middle school students posed no threat to me, but I was educationally and emotionally handicapped where lower elementary children were concerned. Nevertheless, I found myself one day in the second-grade room, ready to perform this necessary chore. My thought was that surely the teacher would sense my feelings of inadequacy and remain in the room; but grateful for a respite, however brief, she soon departed the premises. The children were given sheets with lines on them, containing four pictures. I was to read each question slowly and clearly; the children would then circle the correct answer. Would you believe that I was stumped on the first question? Calmly facing the expectant precious little group, I read, "What does your mother give you to eat when you come home from school?" The four pictures from which they could choose were a pencil, a tree, an apple, and a cat. As the last word of the question left my mouth, a towheaded bit of masculinity shouted, "My momma gives me bologna, but there ain't none on here!" Bedlam ensued.

9   The ninth lesson I learned from my students was to realize that I needed to renew myself often and discipline myself frequently.

Students often challenged me by their interest and aspirations to trod new paths in technology. When the roles of teacher/student were reversed, the injections of humility I received quickly dispelled any notions of condescension that I might have entertained toward a student struggling with the intricacies of proper grammatical usage.

Sometimes, teaching is difficult if those who teach in nearby classrooms do not share your zeal for discipline. Such a person once occupied the room directly across the hall from my room. She was imbued with knowledge in her field of instruction, but she lacked the fortitude to enforce discipline. Sometimes,

I wondered if she felt that she would be more popular with students if her class exemplified the relaxed atmosphere of learning; at other times, I pondered whether she simply valued the unstructured atmosphere too highly. In those days, air-conditioned classrooms were unknown, so all windows were open, and the glass blinds high on the corridor wall of the classrooms were left open for cross ventilation.

One warm day, as I labored to instill in my students a love for the great patriots of pre-Revolutionary days in America, a paper airplane sailed gracefully through the open blinds on my corridor wall. As eloquently as I thought I was presenting this information on giants in America's past, I was no match for this accurately folded white piece of paper that floated to a stop at my feet. My self-control lapsed; my temper flared. I strode to my door, flung it open, marched across the hall through the open door to Mrs. Anything Goes's class, and shouted, "Who threw that airplane?" She stood there amazed as several students shouted the name of the culprit—a lanky star basketball player whose Biblical first name causes one to recall a burning bush and a parted sea. Words signifying my shame should by now be rolling off my pen because I grabbed this student by the arm and propelled him across the hall into my classroom where I demanded of him an apology, which he readily gave. I accepted on behalf of my class, escorted him back to his room, and forthwith took myself to the principal's office where I confessed my transgression of invading another teacher's territory and temporarily taking one of her students. Properly chastised, I returned to my class. I informed the football hero who sat in the first front-row seat that if I ever started out the door in a rage that he was to trip me and sit on me until I regained my self-control.

Most people today probably do not remember a piece of lingerie called a garter belt. It had suspenders that hooked on hose and held them up. Since reading about chastity belts used in the medieval days, I had always equated these two items; panty hose had not appeared in our little hamlet, so a garter belt was somewhat of a necessity. Now, do not expect me to explain the mechanics of what I am about to tell you, but the incident occurred precisely as I shall relate it. One day, as I stood before the class extolling the diplomatic virtues of Benjamin Franklin (the only time I ever interested some of the students in Benjamin Franklin was my expounding on his amorous exploits in Paris!), one of the hooks on a suspender on my garter belt became loose and fell to the floor. There it lay—the only item on the floor between the students and me. They looked at it, looked at each other, and looked at me. They resembled a collection of mimes as they struggled to suppress their laughter. Supporting a sagging stocking, I told them to proceed with their enjoyment of the situation. I had always wanted to assign a wee book entitled *On the Choice of a Mistress and Other Satires and Hoaxes* by Benjamin Franklin, but I had never had the courage or the lack of common sense to do so. After my involuntary display of an intimate object, I was glad I had not ventured farther down the path toward perdition.

A similar incident occurred in another class. Beginning in the midsixties, the faculty members were permitted to wear pantsuits to school. Having been absent for two days, I returned to my classroom to find a note left by the substitute teacher, informing me that one of my classes composed entirely of males had misbehaved. Considering their misbehavior was a black mark on my discipline, I was marching back and forth in front of the class, telling them in certain terms what the consequences of their two-day improper actions would be. I noticed smiles beginning on the faces of the lads in the front rows—smiles that slowly spread all around the room. I had realized that something was amiss, and as all eyes were focused on me, I had a feeling that the something amiss had to do with my apparel. My zipper in the front of my pants had become completely unzipped, and I was so swept up in the frenzy of my tantrum, I had failed to notice.

Once when a friend and I were in London, we went to an ancient pub called Ye Olde Cheshire Cheese, which English dramatist and poet laureate Ben Jonson once frequented. I was so awed to be there; I was perhaps sitting exactly where that revered man of letters had once sat. My friend and I asked our waiter to take a picture of us. Imagine my chagrin and dismay when the developed picture showed me grinning like a Cheshire cat with my necklace hanging gloriously over my left bosom!

> Oh, would some Power the giftie give us
> to see ourselves as others see us!
>
> —Robert Burns, "To a Louse"

In Jackson County, Alabama, is a small town where my husband taught and coached and I taught the second year we were married. We lived in a duplex close to the campus with the vocational agriculture teacher and his elementary-teacher wife. I taught eleventh-grade and twelfth-grade English; I absolutely loved my students, most of whom would easily have earned a degree in *renegado* had such an accolade existed. I felt, after two years there, that I could have served as warden in Alcatraz. If those students had spent as much time studying as they spent thinking of tricks to pull on people, professional ranks would certainly have been strengthened from that corner of the state. Some previous football coaches who had produced championship teams were very popular with the players because they were one of the boys; they had won but had disciplined the players very little.

When Ralph laid down the rules about getting in shape, about laying cigarettes aside, and about passing their courses, the atmosphere darkened. Some of the players just quit, some stayed on obviously to test Ralph's mettle, and some remained to give the season their best efforts. (Please excuse my actions I am about to relate against this background; I was both young and silly.) One afternoon, a football player who had remained on the team and who was riding a beautiful horse came by our apartment to ask if I wanted to ride with him; never even wondering why he was not at practice, up I went! We galloped all over town on both sides of the railroad tracks that bisected the business district. Never once did I think that I was the pawn in this player's game—that he was getting back at my husband in the most unusual way. When Ralph came home from practice, he said, "—was not at practice today, and after practice, someone called from town and said that he and some girl were riding all over everywhere on a horse."

It is said that confession is good for the soul; well, my soul suffered all night because I could not call up the courage to tell Ralph what a dumb thing I had done. After a sleepless night, I related my renegade romp. The player was punished, and I did not receive the Wife of the Week award.

10. The tenth lesson I learned was to listen and give heed to what I heard.

Students often have excellent ideas. Sometimes by our standards, some of these ideas may be outside the realm of orthodoxy, but I learned that the generation gap was best bridged by a compromise of understanding and accepting notions we did not conceive but knew existed. When I genuinely became interested in what the students deemed important, I had a greater opportunity to interest them in what I deemed important. They taught me that lesson well, and I experienced great joy while learning it.

Isn't it amazing how students often hear only a part of what the teacher says? One of my dear friends was teaching American history when she recounted the details of Aaron Burr's killing Alexander Hamilton in a duel. She remarked that this incident was a miscarriage of justice. On the subsequent exam, a question was "How did Alexander Hamilton die?" One half-alert chair occupant answered, "He had a miscarriage."

One of the favorite creative answers I received came from a student who obviously had not read the assigned biographical sketch on Mark Twain. To my inquiry "In what state was Mark Twain born?" he confidently wrote, "In a state of nudity." One of my history students proudly proclaimed *Huguenots* to be French prostitutes while another defined a *scarab* as a scared beetle rather than a sacred one. I hoped that was a spelling error. When we read *Silas Marner*, I made vocabulary sheets to familiarize the students with the language of the times. They were to be able to spell and define the words. Imagine my surprise when one student (who had obviously had his mind on something other than the lesson when the word was defined) wrote that an *ostler* was "one who ostles."

During my first year of teaching, a young lady in a seventh-grade world history class paid much more attention to the boys than she did to my teaching. We had Visitors' Day when parents came and sat by their students. This girl's mother sat by her. Realizing that she knew very little about the Roman Empire, which we had been studying, I asked her the simplest question I could. We had fully discussed the size of the Roman Empire and the fact that the Romans built good roads so they could move their armies quickly from one place to another, so I chose for her question, "Why did the Romans build good roads throughout the empire?" Without a moment's hesitation, she answered, "So they would not tear up their cars." Don't you wonder what her mother thought I had been teaching?

In the early fifties when I began teaching, the phrase "School days, school days, dear old golden rule days" certainly ran true because there were many strictly enforced rules for the students, one of which prohibited chewing gum. What a fascination rules have for youth! Many times, thinking of ways to circumvent the establishment, students spend valuable time; their resistance to authority is perhaps as characteristic of a teenager as their complaints about lunchroom food. My classes knew my policy that my classes were gum-free. I would not even have entertained the notion that someone had gum in his or her mouth but did not chew! I was so proud of the punishment I had devised for this offense that I could hardly wait for some person to violate the rule. In my exuberance to maintain authority, I failed to consider how much of the culprit's time I was guilty of wasting. I had each person detected chewing gum to draw one hundred gum wrappers complete with small print and symbols. Think of the time these perpetrators wasted on this penal artwork when they could have been studying. How I wish some wise teacher had taken me aside and spoken softly to me about constructive methods of punishment. Later in my teaching career, I began to assign memory work, which I considered nourishment for brain activity with the hope that magnificent words, phrases, and sentences would serve the students far better than reproducing gum wrappers.

CHAPTER TWO

Superintendents and Principals:
Loud Thunder

Superintendents are the chief executive officers of the school system; principals are the chief executive officers of the schools. Superintendents outrank principals; principals outrank faculty and staff who outrank maintenance personnel. During my teaching career, I was fortunate to work for (in some instances), with (in other instances) some excellent administrators; one or two principals might honestly have considered me their number one reason to contemplate early retirement.

May I share with you some lessons I learned from my superintendants and principals?

1. I learned to hold steadfast to my standards, whatever the personal price might be.

There were times when a coach backed by the principal caused a problem when he tried to put athletics above academics. Such a case occurred the fifth year I taught. A senior who was extremely talented in the game of basketball developed the opinion that he was such an athletic asset to the school that he could ignore the rudiments of composition and the artistry of literature. This seed of self-aggrandizement was nourished by the basketball coach who attempted to bully me into giving this boy a passing grade in English the second six weeks of school so he would be eligible to play ball. Part of this coach's argument was that composition and literature played no practical part in life, so what good were they anyway? Perhaps I might have buckled under had the coach been more appreciative of my previous efforts to help the student; he was in a study hall that I supervised, and I had offered many times to help him.

Alas, he had found the written word of *Field and Stream* much more enjoyable than his studies and had always refused my help. So I refused to change the grade whereupon I was summoned to the inner sanctum where I was questioned as to who was the ultimate authority at the school—the principal or the teacher. Reluctantly, I gave the answer the principal wanted to hear. I was then ordered to change the grade; I refused. The principal changed it anyway. Right then, I told him that I would not teach for him another year. He called my husband to report my impertinence.

(Note: Later, the young man came to my home and apologized. I taught at a different school the next year.)

2.   I learned to appreciate administrative support.

Walking the halls of a high school can be an enlightening experience. One is likely to see T-shirts emblazoned with various sayings and pictures. Normally, they are not *R*-rated. However, one day as I faced a horde or students moving in the opposite direction from me, I noticed a student's T-shirt that proclaimed in heavy black letters KEEP ON F—. When he realized that I had seen the shirt, he ran. I went after him, but he escaped, so I went to the principal's office to report the violation to the administration. The principal ridiculed me, telling me that I had misread the saying—that many T-shirts had KEEP ON TRUCKING on the front. I tried to tell him that I knew what I had seen; what this student was advocating had little to do with a truck except a rhyme scheme. The principal continued to tell me that a student would never wear such a shirt. I went to my class, gave them a writing assignment so I could be absent for a few minutes, and began a systematic search for the pervert. I found him in geometry class, went back to report my successful search to the principal, and returned to my class, smug in the knowledge that had triumphed over the vulgarity of the student as well as the obstinacy of the principal, who admitted the letters said what I had thought and administered proper discipline.

Motorcycles may not fit the image most teachers like to project, but even when I was in high school, I loved riding motorcycles, and that love has continued throughout my life. Riding in the Trail of Tears ride in 2001 was a highlight for me. I am giving this background to explain my behavior when I was a young teacher at Athens High School. As I started to walk home down Beaty Street, a student on a Harley stopped and asked if I wanted a ride. Oh, I did! I did! I pulled my skirt up as gracefully as I could, slung my schoolbag over my shoulder, and was ready to roll. Would you believe that the next afternoon in the faculty meeting, an aged lady teacher (without any warning to me) brought up the fact that she had seen me get on the back of a motorcycle with a student? Almost brought to tears by this unexpected and—I thought—totally undeserved attack, I could only sit there. My principal, a true gentleman of the Old South, suggested to this battle-axe that she might try doing something to establish a better relationship with her students. My tears were converted into giggles as I pictured her astraddle a Harley!

  3.   I learned to question when I did not understand.

Perhaps one reason another principal and I worked well together was that each of us had a temper that displayed itself in unexpected tantrums; at times those of us who witnessed his spontaneous spasms of temper never knew what set him off. One Friday after school, a faculty meeting was scheduled in the library. Only a person who has taught (even though he or she loved every minute of it) realizes the beauty of the word *Friday*. As we sat and waited for the principal to appear, we were discussing our triumphs and tragedies of the past week quietly. Suddenly, the principal strode into the room, threw a heavy book upon the counter, and shouted at us, "Which of you clowns thinks you are Flip Wilson? Well, I don't think you are so damn funny!" He wheeled around and left the room.

For several minutes, stunned by his performance, we simply sat there. Then the group decided that I should go to him and seek the source of his irritation. Actually, I figured that I was probably the one responsible for his wrath, though I could think of no recent erring on my part. I knocked on his office door and entered after a blunt "Come in." He told me that someone had written a smart remark on a list he had sent around for chaperones for a school dance. He never apologized for his bizarre behavior, and we never knew the identity of the culprit. I confess I did not ask him "Was it I?" because I had forgotten what I had written.

  4.   I learned to realize that mistakes are made on all levels of the educational
       hierarchy.

Nowadays, I attribute my absent-mindedness to senility. In the midsixties, I had no such excuse. One year, we had an unusual assortment of slothful sophomore males. They appeared to be most adept at locking the French teacher in a large book cabinet in her room or in skillfully diverting a copy of a test from the mimeograph machine (how many of you remember this object?) or in composing bawdy lyrics to a Robert Frost poem or in seeing who could offer the most blatant falsehood for missing homework. In a moment of temporary derangement, the school counselor had placed thirty of these malefactors in one of my English classes. They were such adorable rogues that I could hardly stay aggravated at their antics; frankly, at times I experienced difficulty in not praising their creativity, criminally inclined as it was.

One day, I requested that they convene in the Little Theater on the following day as I wished to divide them into groups for brainstorming. Evidently, I promptly forgot giving them these instructions because I did not make note of it on my schedule. The next day when the class-changing bell announced that it was time for the parade of these perpetrators into my room, no one appeared. Not a single annoying adolescent appeared. My first and last thoughts were the same: the entire group had skipped my class. They had always supported one another, so it was easy for me to believe they had acted as a unit. In a state of panic, I rushed to the principal's office and denounced the missing demons. The principal and I had called the parents of about one-third of the class to report the truancy when an office assistant discovered the class intact in the Little Theater. They had wondered where I was. My embarrassment was no match for the principal's wrath.

5. I learned to support the administration in *most* incidents involving students.

My brother-in-law was head football coach and assistant principal part of the time I taught at Athens High School. One spring when streaking (some people call it flashing) was in fashion, we enjoyed an amusing mistake on the part of one of the teachers. Some young man clad only in footwear and a raincoat had been making forays at various places on the campus. At a major league baseball game during this time, a bare-to-the-bone individual jumped from the stands and streaked across first base headed for second. An alert and observant organist immediately began playing "Is That All There Is?"

As a footnote to what I am about to relate, I should tell you that my friend and I had taken some students to New Orleans to see the King Tut Exhibit. As we walked in the French Quarter, we met a man wearing a trench coat, his hairy legs protruding. Before we realized that his attire was suggestive, he jerked the coat open to reveal his private parts (of which he must have been inordinately proud) covered by a diaper on which was printed HOME OF THE WHOPPER. So school administrators, faculty, staff, and students were aware of streaking. In fact, we faculty had been told to watch for any strange happenings and report them at once to the office.

At the time, we had several student teachers on campus. His first day there, one student teacher wearing a suit and a trench coat mistakenly opened the door to the ladies' lounge, whereupon a history teacher seated there saw only the trench coat, jumped up, and screamed. He quickly shut the door and began a fast movement down the hall, hotly pursued by the aging teacher shouting, "The streaker! The streaker!" My brother-in-law heard the commotion, ran from his office, collared the hapless student teacher whom he had never seen before, and propelled him into the principal's office. There the mistake was rectified, but I often wondered if that young man continued to follow a career in education.

Why do students love graffiti? Many years ago, the daughter of a wonderful local preacher, who had since moved, was reprimanded for an action she did not realize was a violation. Several days later, the janitors informed the principal—whom I shall refer to as Mr. Doe—that graffiti in bright green paint adorned the walls of both the upstairs and downstairs girls' bathrooms. Mr. Doe was sorely beset when he viewed the graffiti because it boldly proclaimed "Mr. Doe uses a night light." Now most males, I believe, would love to have had a chapter in John Kennedy's *Profiles in Courage* dedicated to them, so to have his courage impugned by such graffiti was about more than Mr. Doe could stand. He began an all-out campaign to discover the writer of such an insult. Then through no fault of my own, I entered into the picture. The student who exercised her artistic talent to send this derogatory message came to me and said she needed to talk with me. Never once had I suspected her of the misdeed; she felt better, and I felt worse when she shifted part of her burden to me. I convinced her to put an end to the principal's agony and suffer the consequences. She valiantly did this.

6. I learned to accept the certainty that, at times, I was a thorn in a principal's side without trying to be. Had I tried, I would have been a bramble.

The last years that I taught at Athens High School, my office was in the library. That office was my solace one day when, with my arms loaded with books and papers, I fell in the lunchroom in full view of a fascinated audience. Hastily I jumped to my feet, thanked the students who had come to help me, gathered my gear, and fled to my office. My friend Barbara, the librarian, came to meet me as I entered the library. "Help me to my office and close the door," I said. "I have killed myself." I assessed the damage to my bruised body and attempted to compose my wounded pride. I suppose I have always liked being the center of attention, but sprawled awkwardly on the lunchroom floor was not the position I sought.

That same office was my nemesis one Friday in the early fall when a student whose grandfather was a farmer brought me a beautiful watermelon. Forgetting to take it home, I left it in my office all weekend. Would you believe that it exploded? My knowledge of agricultural products being greatly limited, I was completely at a loss to explain the bits of red, white, and green that littered my office walls, the furniture, and the floors. My retired-military principal was not amused. It was as though he thought that somehow I had rigged this unusual bursting of the product of the vine.

So many students hear different drummers. Henry David Thoreau stated, "If a man does not keep pace with his companions, perhaps it is because he hears a different drummer. Let each man step to the music that he hears." In the 1970s, when some male students wished to wear their hair long, dress in weird outfits, and display earrings in one ear or maybe both, school authorities got up in arms. The superintendent of education called a special faculty meeting to address this situation and try to arrive at a solution. My smart-a—genes shoved aside my common-sense genes as I listened to countless criticisms of these students. It was my opinion that they would have forsaken these deviations had we not made such an issue of them. My mouth, again, got me in trouble as I stood and addressed the group with this startling statement: "I do not care if a student comes to my class buck naked with an earring in each ear if he has a good attitude and wants to learn." So much for my good standing with the administrative contingent after that exhibition. Later, a faculty member at a local college told me about a similar meeting they had held about having a dress code. One of the first faculty members to speak was a lady renowned for her unusual attire. She rose majestically to aver, "I, for one, am opposed to any oddity in dress." We just don't see ourselves as others see us.

When I was interviewed in 1963 for the team-teaching experience, the superintendent of education conducting the interview asked what I considered even then rather personal questions: "Do you smoke?" "Do you drink?" "Do you use profanity?" Later, how I wished I had thought to respond to each question with a question "Do you?" I left after one year because the principal and I simply did not see events in the same light. The school had a new library, so the principal made a very logical suggestion regarding Christmas presents that year. He planted the idea that the best gifts students and teachers could give each other were books for the library with inscriptions as to who was being honored by the gift. Everyone was enthusiastic about selecting books that were representative of different individuals. I chaired the faculty committee that was to select a gift for the principal. Thinking that we were complying with his express wishes, we brought Carl Sandburg's magnificent biography of Abraham Lincoln to put in the library in his honor. He was not pleased. His wife phoned me to say that he wanted a smoking jacket and that he had dropped several subtle hints to that effect. He expressed later his disappointment in the faculty gift.

CHAPTER THREE

Apt Answers, Relevant Replies, and Pertinent Put-Downs

Humor and wit are tremendous teaching tools. Many a stumbling block has been turned into a stepping-stone by the use of one of these qualities. Humor appeals to a sense of the ludicrous such as a situation comedy on television whereas wit is more likely to appeal to intellectual power or reason such as the banter that existed between Winston Churchill and some of his colleagues, notably George Bernard Shaw.

May I share with you some lessons I learned from administrators, students, and others about the value of an apt answer or a relevant reply or even a pertinent put-down?

1. I learned that quickly putting together an appropriate answer might relieve a potentially bad situation; a witty reply would sometimes serve a better purpose than a stern rebuke.

Haven't you always wanted to have a wonderfully suitable comeback when you really needed it? Often, I have envied those people who could participate in conversations laced with great repartee. Such a one was about a ragamuffin (defined by *Webster* as a disreputable tatterdemalion—what a splendid word!) about eight years old who, early one summer morning, knocked on the front door of the home of an elderly Athenian lady. This dowager was accustomed to having her morning cup of tea without interruption, so she opened the door with some anger already building. When she saw the unhygienic lad obviously from that section of North Athens known as Booger Town, she thundered at him, "What in hell do you want?" Not one bit dismayed by this large lady in her negligee, the urchin answered, "I wanted to mow your damn yard!" And so he did all summer!

The eight years that I taught at Calhoun Community College, I was also director of the Honors Program. Faculty members were gracious to recommend potential Honors Program participants. One student who came highly recommended was an Israeli boy who rode a motorcycle each day from a nearby city. On the way to Calhoun one day, he was involved in an accident that resulted in his having a broken ankle; nevertheless, he continued to ride his motorcycle to school. He and I soon became friends; conversing with him was a pure joy because he was knowledgeable and well traveled.

One day when he dropped by my office, I was too busy for conversation. Not wishing to offend him because of my schedule, I said to him, "Come back tomorrow about noon, and I shall take you to lunch."

The next day at around noon, he appeared. The first words he spoke to me were "Mrs. Brett, how old are you?"

Instead of telling him my age, I replied, "That is a rude question. Why would you ask me that?"

Quickly he responded, "Mrs. Brett, are you trying to pick me up?"

For once in my life, I was so proud to retort, "Look, I may try to pick someone up sometime, but I doubt very much that it will be a crippled Israeli riding a motorcycle!" My pride in that remark violated all political correctness procedures—a display of snobbery and anti-Semitic feelings not at all intended!

In one of my Humanities classes was a lovely student named Joy. One day, just as class was beginning, she came to me in great anxiety to say that she had left her purse in the library. Students were not allowed in the halls without passes. As I was very busy, I hastily scribbled, "Joy to the library. E. Brett." She returned with her purse and a note that read, "Peace to Humanities. B. Searcy."

Another student who spent time with us was from Iran. He was very handsome; his dark good looks captivated the girls and irritated the boys. One night, he rang our doorbell rather late and breathlessly requested sanctuary because several discarded Lotharios from Limestone County were hot on his trail. They deemed him the cause of their romantic troubles. Our language fascinated him. He asked, "Why do you say 'How do you do?' How do you do what?"

Late one Friday afternoon, I was in a local grocery store as were many other people. There were long lines at each checkout counter. Working at the first checkout line was one of my senior students—the very essence of civility and courtesy. The store manager was a middle-aged lady—the very essence of noncivility and rudeness. The student had just moved up from stocking shelves to working the cash register, so he was a bit nervous. When he totaled the bill of the lady directly in front of me, he hit a wrong button or two, and her receipt rolled out with an astronomical amount on it. The customer waited patiently and graciously as the student summoned the lady manager. She descended upon the hapless cashier with the fury of a summer storm. She ranted on and on. I was so sorry for him that I leaned forward and said, "He just made a little mistake." By this time, the incident was providing entertainment for several shoppers.

She wheeled around to face me and shouted, "Listen, you may think you run Athens High School, but you don't run Kroger!"

I was so surprised at her attack on me that I barely managed to say to the cashier, "Well, at least I got her off you and on me."

For many years, I taught Sunday school to the ninth-grade through the twelfth-grade youth at First United Methodist Church in Athens. Knowing that it is not easy for offspring to be taught by their parents whether at church or at school, I dropped back to teach seventh and eighth graders when our son Dan became a freshman. During my college education, I was never offered a course in "Overcoming Student Rudeness," so I was totally unprepared for what awaited me. One boy was surely the Grand Dragon of the Rudeness Brigade. When he continued to talk and amuse his cohorts even when I was talking, my already thread-bare patience completely collapsed, whereupon I took the young hellion out in the hall and said to him, "Harken, heed, and listen. If you don't correct your behavior, I shall bring you back out here and spank you!" Immediately, I felt a tap on my shoulder, and the angelic voice of the precious octogenarian lady who served as superintendent of the Sunday school came to me, "Elizabeth, remember that you are in the House of the Lord!" I knew her message would be dire when she addressed me as Elizabeth instead of Lib.

My husband and I were so delighted when Dan and his wife told us they were expecting a baby. Soon thereafter, Ralph and I went to Panama City, Florida, to visit Momma Tee, Ralph's mother. We could hardly wait to tell her the news. For some reason, on the way there, Ralph had gotten irritated with me (can you imagine?). Momma Tee happily heard the news and then asked, "If it's a girl, will they name the baby for Lib?"

Ralph answered his elderly elegant mother with a statement I could scarcely believe I was hearing: "If they do, they'll have to call her smart-a—!"

2. I learned that sarcasm disguised thinly as wit should never be used as a weapon to wound others.

One of my great desires was to travel to Europe, but teachers married to coaches had to seek some means of financial assistance to travel in the United States, much less abroad. In the mid-1960s, I had an opportunity to go to Europe by chaperoning a group of students, each of whom I knew well. A friend accompanied me as we cautiously shepherded eighteen soon-to-be high school seniors on one of those "If it is Tuesday, it must be Belgium" tours. We flew from Huntsville to New York to Brussels. When the plane landed, some of the students pointed out a wee man with an umbrella on his arm, somewhat reminiscent of Neville Chamberlain in earlier years. A woman and another couple stood with him. One of my students said that he had just come up with their group and said, "I hope you little sons of bitches had a good time on the plane last night. You kept us awake!"

The rudder temper, which I inherited from my momma, surged through my veins, arteries, and capillaries. I marched over to him and accosted him. "Sir, I am the teacher with these sons of bitches. Do you wish you register a complaint with me?" The delightful outcome of this episode was that those two couples attached themselves to our group for the entire two weeks. We enjoyed their company immensely and felt very secure with four more adults with us. Occasionally, the wee man who was an architect in Charleston, South Carolina, would disagree with something I told the group. For example, when we were in Cologne, Germany, we stood before the magnificent Cologne Cathedral and marveled at the fact that Allied bombers in WWII had destroyed much of the area around it, but it had sustained little damage. I said to the students, "That this cathedral was spared was probably because of the grace of God." "Not so," the wee man retorted. "It was undoubtedly the skill of the Allied bombardiers."

When Dan was in kindergarten, one of the little boys who attended was a biter. He had bitten several children before he "tasted" Dan. In checking the degree of cleanliness that he had attained during his bath, I was very disconcerted to see a large bite mark on his shoulder. At once, I phoned the teacher and explained (I hope in a courteous fashion) that Dan would not return to kindergarten if the other child continued to bite. I was and am of the opinion that bites are dangerous to the "bitee." The next day, a friend of mine drove carpool to kindergarten. She related to me that when the boys got into her station wagon, her child said, "Today the teacher told—if he bit Dan anymore that he [the biter] could not come back to kindergarten. I guess it won't matter if he eats the rest of us up!"

3. I learned that the twenty-six letters of the alphabet can frequently be used to sweeten the conversation so that others will feel better about themselves.

"A sound mind in a healthy body" was the philosophy of the Greek intellectuals. Some of us seem to equate *healthy* with *shapely*. When Ralph and I married over fifty years ago, I weighed ninety pounds. With the passing of the years came the adding of the pounds; but even with a large bosom, a greatly expanded waist, and much larger hips, I never developed a posterior. Having seen a Frederick's of Hollywood advertisement in a Nashville paper, I decided to purchase myself a false bottom. My friend and I traveled the hundred miles north to try to make a buy that would accentuate my shape. Have you ever seen a false bottom? This particular model was a pair of thick panties with hard shoulder-pad material molded to the shape of a bottom and sewed in the back of the panties (perhaps they are much improved today). I secured my size and retired to the dressing room to try on this item that I hoped would cause my clothes to drape in a sexy way over my rear. I envisioned being ogled as I walked away from a group or an individual. I redressed and exited the dressing room. When she saw me, my friend literally fell off her chair from laughing. Even a clumsy waiter could have set a tray on my protuberance. My thoughts turned to my friend's reaction to my appearance. If she reacted in such a way, how would my students respond? As I pictured their mirth, I decided to make do with the body I had.

Sometimes a teacher will suffer public rebukes that will cause him or her to be less harsh in reprimanding students. Once, I was conducting a seminar on teaching techniques for several Boeing employees who were about to begin teaching personal improvement courses. There were approximately thirty people in the class whose positions of employment ranged from accountants to engineers. They filed into the room and sat down. A middle-aged lady in a green dress was seated in the front seat of the middle row. After I introduced myself and explained what I planned to do in the three days allocated for the instruction, I asked if anyone had a question. Immediately, she raised her hand and said that she did not have a question but that she would like to make a statement. With obvious indignation, she announced that she, as an accountant, was far too busy to waste three days on this nonsense—that anybody could teach and that this so-called instruction was totally unnecessary. Talk about a good beginning for me; I was already in a very different environment on an educational level (in some opinions!) inferior to those I had been hired to instruct. My spirits fell, but my determination rose. I worked unusually hard to make my presentations pleasant and practical. She wrote me a note of apology at the end of the session.

4. I learned that in the teaching atmosphere, there is absolutely no place for the studied insult.

When my friend and I took the students to Europe, one student was a beautiful girl from out in the county near Athens. She was beautiful without realizing how gorgeous she was. She attracted the attention of males affiliated with several countries. In Venice, Italy, we ate dinner at the hotel where we were staying. A handsome young Italian waiter could hardly perform his duties because his dark eyes kept straying to her. When dinner and the evening's entertainment were over, she came to my friend and me and showed us a note in which he had requested her room number; he had left the note on her plate. Laughing, she reported that she had given him our room number. I wish I could report that he came and we two old ladies opened the door in our rollers and robes, but somehow, he must have discovered the ruse. Often, I have wondered if these two beautiful people enjoyed a late-night tryst after throwing us off the track.

One of the male students with us requested permission not to attend the floor show at the Moulin Rouge; his excuse being that the near-nudity would throw his health off balance. He insisted that this bit of Parisian frivolity would most certainly place him in harm's way, so we granted his request. A couple of days later, we engaged a young French girl as a guide to Versailles. She boarded our bus, and we stared in amazement. She was fashionably attired in black leather pants, a very sheer black shirt, and no bra. At once, the young man who had refused to go to the Moulin Rouge informed my friend that he would have a heart attack if he had to stay on the bus and be exposed to body bareness. We were determined that he would absorb a bit of French history, so we bade him sit in the back of the bus and keep his eyes averted from the sensuous sensation in the front.

A precious lady was a substitute teacher at the local high school for many years. Back in those glory days, faculty members had assigned parking spaces. When she first began substituting, she did not realize that we had spaces numbered and assigned; she evidently took a liking to my spot because she parked in my place every day for a week. She drove a blue Volkswagen. Each of those days when I arrived at school, that little blue car sat proudly, never knowing that it was infringing on my space. On Monday of the next week, there sat Blue Car again. I took action. Not knowing whose car it was, I addressed a very sarcastic note to Blue Car and put it under a windshield wiper. Imagine my dismay when this precious lady came to my room the next morning to offer an apology on behalf of Blue Car. A bit of investigation on my part would have resulted in my not being embarrassed because I would gladly have relinquished my space to that lady.

Just before Christmas several years ago, I was in Kroger grocery when I saw a faculty member from our local college. She looked like a model always. I greeted her warmly since I had not seen her in a while. "Merry Christmas! I am glad to see you!" I said. I could tell from her reaction that she did not recognize me, so I said, "I'm Lib Brett."

Quickly she exclaimed, "My goodness! You have gotten so fat and gray that I never would have known you!" I do hope she never realized how she wounded my pride in the vicinity of the tropical fruits.

Calhoun Community College offered off-campus courses at several sites. One fall quarter, I taught a Western civilization course two nights a week at Lee High School. A retired army officer with a heightened view of himself was a member of the class. He was argumentative and rude; obviously, he resented the fact that a female was in control of the class. He was absent for two sessions (one week), so when he returned, I told him that I had missed him. He replied that he had been in the hospital with heart trouble. When I said that I was sorry to hear that news, sarcastically he answered, "Well, you ought to be sorry. You were the cause of my being in the hospital." Then I suggested that he drop the course as it would benefit him little if he departed the planet, but he persevered.

At the very end of each course, students evaluated the instructors on standard evaluation sheets that they did not sign. Instructors were rated in several areas on a scale of 1 to 5, with 5 being the best. One of my sheets gave me twenty-four 1s. The twenty-fifth question was "Would you recommend this instructor to your friends?" On this particular sheet, the answer was yes, so I always figured the army retiree gave me all those low marks and that he wanted his friends to endure what he had survived.

Humiliation, reducing a student to a lower position in the eyes of his or her peers, should never be used in the classroom; and most assuredly, one faculty member should never degrade another faculty member in front of a class. Such an abasement occurred one day at Athens High School when a teacher of English—who vented her anger at inept students by viciously kicking the Coke machine in the teachers' lounge and who frightened teachers and students alike with her terrible temper tantrums—did an awful deed. A fellow faculty member had written her a note to explain why a student was tardy to class. She copied the note word for word on the board, signed the writer's name, and then corrected it with great slashes of white chalk. How long do you suppose it took the students in her class that day to transmit her misdeed to the outside world? The corrected colleague was enraged, and her students were embarrassed; but she saw no wrongdoing in her action.

5.   I learned that rebukes or corrections we adults sometimes need may come from unexpected sources.

One benefit of teaching, which I enjoyed immensely, was getting to know some of the foreign students who attended the local college. One intelligent and articulate young man from South Africa was quite impressive. Having been educated by British missionaries, he spoke in an eloquent way. We first met him at a church supper at the end of which he needed a ride to his dormitory. We offered to transport him. Ralph was driving, I was in the passenger seat, and he sat directly behind Ralph. As he was explained how he had arrived in our Alabama hamlet from his faraway home, he paused. Ralph thought the conversation was over, so he began to talk. Immediately, the young man leaned forward, tapped Ralph on the shoulder, and said, "Pardon me, sir. I am still conversing with madam." A pertinent put-down by a polite passenger!

He spent the Easter holidays with us that year. After church that Sunday, our entire family convened at my sister's river home for our annual egg hunt and horseshoe tournament. His amazement was unbounded as he witnessed the antics of Momma's six grandsons as they unleashed their energy in pursuit of rare ringers and hidden eggs. When he graduated from Athens State, he invited Ralph and me to attend as his family. I was ever so proud!

Frequently, we teachers were given opportunities to evaluate ourselves in the hope that we would recognize our flaws and correct them. On an evaluation sheet one day, I wrote that I was doing all I knew to do in order to make my classes relevant and interesting. Imagine my chagrin when I was called for my evaluation by the principal and was told "Perhaps you could work on developing a sense of humility."

One day when my nephew Mike was about three years old, we passed McConnell Funeral Home on our way home. There were several cars there, so Mike asked me what the building was. When I told him that it was a funeral home and explained its function, he inquired, "Lib, when you die, will you go to heaven?"

I replied, "I certainly hope so."

Mike then asked, "Will you be an angel?"

Enthusiastically, I answered, "I hope so."

He thought for a few seconds, then he looked directly at me and said, "I've never seen an old angel!" He could not reconcile the image of a cherub with that of an aging aunt.

One of my friends at the high school had a young nephew whose mother brought him with her when she picked my friend up after school. After the bell rang, this four-year-old would frequently come to my room because I kept treats that I shared with him. One day when he came, I was so busy helping some students that I just hugged him and forgot to give him a treat. About fifteen minutes later, as I was about to exit the building, I saw him standing by the door. As I approached, he grabbed a textbook, opened it, and pretended to read "That little black boy went to see the white teacher, and she did not give him a thing." What a wonderful way to remind me of my inadequate acknowledgment of his visit to my room.

CHAPTER FOUR

Dirty Haviland and Crumpled Damask
or
A Bit Soiled but Redeemable

No person-administrator, faculty member, staff member, or student has mistake insurance or error insurance. Some mistakes are easily set right, though a cup of courage may be the ingredient needed for the confession and atonement.

May I share with you some lessons I learned about making mistakes and drawing on the reserve of integrity and civility to correct them?

1. Confucius said, "The cautious seldom err." I learned to think (most of the time!) before I spoke, to weigh my words to determine whether they held the potential for wounding a fellow inhabitant of this orb.

The first year I taught, I was nineteen years old. I was so happy to be teaching on the junior-high level in a Limestone County school. In those days, hitchhiking was common and, as far as we knew, safe. My fiancé Ralph Brett was visiting from Florida, his objective being the courtship of Elizabeth. We were riding around when we saw a young man thumbing, so we offered him a ride. As he seemed very ill at ease, I tried to converse with him; I told him where I taught. His face brightened, and he asked, "Do you know Sally Jones [real name not used]?" I replied that I did know who she was. He then remarked, "She is about to get married." In a moment of foot-in-mouth seizure, I inquired as to who in the world would marry such a tacky girl. He said, "Me, and I want to get out right here." I was so ashamed of myself that I vowed to weigh my words carefully ere I spoke again.

Once, a dear friend of mine invited me to go with her and a very prominent lady to a Broadway play in Huntsville. In those days, I was teaching Humanities and college-prep English, so I was exhausted mentally and physically at the end of the day. I got into the car, and the prominent lady graciously asked, "How are you?"

My tongue swept my brain out of the picture, and I replied, "I am just as tired as I look. Are you?"

"No, honey," she answered. "I am just old."

Later in the darkness of the theater, my aggravated friend whispered to ask me why I said what I did. She insisted that my response to "How are you?" bordered on insolence and rudeness. I had no defense.

I finished my career as an educator at Calhoun Community College, where I was directory of the Honors Program as well as an instructor in the program. Someone who knew how I admired Mikhail Baryshnikov's work gave me a black-and-white life-size poster of him, which I hung on the back of my office door. Unless the door was closed, the poster could not be seen. One of my students had a teenaged brother who was mentally challenged; she brought him to see me one day. As they entered, he shut the door, and my poster was visible. He excitedly exclaimed, "There's Gorbachev!"
Immediately, I responded with, "You ninny! You know Gorbachev does not dance in the ballet! That's Baryshnikov!"

The minute the words left the privacy of my mouth, I remembered that his sister had told me about his mentality. But before I could do or say anything, he threw his arms around me and said, "Mrs. Brett, thank you for calling me a ninny. I know that I am different, but everyone else tries to ignore it." Oh, my shame!

Students often need help and guidance in other areas than academics. Once, I taught a young lady who was highly intelligent with a pleasing personality. She was an only child who enjoyed the fruits of her parents' love and wealth. She apparently had everything she wanted but a sweetheart. When she confessed this need to me, I decided to try to help her attain some affection from the male gender. She wore nice clothes, but she was a bit lacking in style. In my vast knowledge of preludes to romance, I determined that what she needed was a complete makeover. It was my opinion that a dramatic change in her appearance would cause boys to notice her. Totally receptive to my suggestion, she had her hair cut and styled in a shape that accentuated her high cheek bones, she exchanged her scholarly spectacles for contact lenses, and she and her mother shopped for and purchased apparel designed to highlight her best features. Both she and I were delighted with the results, but one day when she appeared in my office, I spotted what I considered to be a major faux pas—an offense against my standards of style. She had on stockings with reinforced toes and casual sandals. I chastised her and instructed her to go forthwith to the restroom and remove the stockings. She did, we chatted briefly, and she left to go to class. I did not realize that our division secretary, a precious person whom I love and adore, had overheard my admonishing the student, so I was absolutely chagrined when she called out "Ta-da!" and stuck her reinforced-stocking sandal-clad foot around the corner of my office door. I was so embarrassed as I tried to explain that my ideas concerning stockings and sandals might not coincide with those of the fashion world.

Humiliation can occur on a one-to-one basis with only two people involved. My memory cells resurrect one painful episode that transpired during the basketball career of one of my nephews. *Inept* was a word far too strong to describe the coaching techniques of the dapper gentleman who filled the position of the basketball coach. Because of the intimidating presence of other family members, I had held my escalating displeasure at his inability to manage the team in check, but finally one night when other pressures of the day had compounded my frustration, I determined to have my say to the coach. It was as though opportunity actually called to me; no one was around but the coach, who was gathering his pad and some papers. Other people had left, my family had all gone to the restroom, and the team had gone to the dressing room. Suddenly I was out of the bleachers. I approached the coach and identified myself as the aunt of my nephew, and then I announced, "Coach—, I do believe I could read a book on basketball and do a better job of coaching than you do." Instantly, I was contrite, but the words were gone from my control; they hung in that sweat-scented air of the gymnasium—hung there between a well-dressed Southern gentleman and an aunt whose new perm caused her to resemble an aged Orphan Annie. The coach wore an amazed look—a look that seemed to ask "Who is this demented female?" Having displayed qualities that would have earned me the position of Poster Person for Rudeness, I quickly left the gymnasium to await other family members in the hall. I was so ashamed of what I had done that I told no one. I thought my shameful secret might be safe, but it was not to be. A few days later, my nephew called me to tell me the coach had asked him if his aunt would be attending the next game. He wondered why the coach would ask him such a question. So I confessed, but I never apologized. Alas! I sorely needed a strong dose of civility.

2.   I learned that students love knowing that the teacher has made a mistake; therefore, "I don't know" as an honest reply will carry more weight with students than submitting to hypocrisy and attempting to devise an answer.

The last year I taught at Athens High School, construction began on a new gymnasium. I was going down the hall to the office when I saw a young man standing at the water fountain. He was a nice-looking lad, and I was about to make a friendly remark to him, though I did not know him. The school was large enough that it was difficult for a teacher to know all the students. Suddenly, my eyes were riveted to his T-shirt front where a personal testimony was vulgarly proclaimed: "I like peace and quiet so give me a piece and I'll be quiet!" I touched his arm and said, "Let's go to the office." He began protesting, but with great dignity because of the indignity he had thrust upon me, I hushed him. I escorted him to the office where, with the exuberance of a bounty hunter claiming his reward, I instructed him to show his shirt to the principal. With embarrassment and reluctance, he stood so that the vulgarity was visible.

Then he began his explanation by saying, "I am a construction worker on the new gym. I came in here to get a drink of water, and this lady grabbed me!" Needless to say, the principal chastised him for wearing such a shirt in the school building, and I left the office with righteous indignation assuaged.

During my first year of teaching, I had several embarrassing situations, not the very least of which occurred in the lunchroom one day. A gentleman who was married to my fourth-grade teacher, whom I adored, came to Clements High School to show rings from the Balfour Company to the seniors. When he finished his presentation, he asked the principal if he might have permission to say hello to me. The principal told him that I was in the lunchroom with my students, so he came there to see me. I had just gotten my tray on which I had a bowl of bologna soup. I was delighted to see my friend, and in my exuberance, I dropped my spoon off my tray. I had already opened my half pint of chocolate milk. While my friend was bent to retrieve my spoon, the milk slid off my tray, hit him squarely in the back of his starched white shirt, and cascaded to the lunchroom floor. Wouldn't you think that was enough embarrassment for one fledgling teacher on a winter's day? Something else awaited me.

The weather was unusually severe; ice and snow covered the campus. Some of the older boys had poured water on the walkway on the north side of the building to make a slide. This incident occurred in the early fifties when people did not have easy access to amusement parks. This same afternoon, a gentleman from the State Department of Education made a visit to the school. The bell rang to signal the end of the school day; several of the boys who had made the slide came to my room to invite me to participate in their activity. Oh, how I wanted to participate! So I did! One student, who is now a doting grandpa, took me by the hand. We got a running start, had a thrilling slide, and fell prone at the feet of the principal and his visitor. My heart almost stopped as my principal stepped around me without acknowledging my presence. I knew he would have a few words for me the next day. How I wished these two episodes had occurred on a Friday; being a preacher, my principal might have been softened by Sunday.

Now to the bologna soup. During this same period of time, my mouth got me in trouble again. Caustically and carelessly one day, I remarked in the presence of a small group of students that perhaps a boycott of the lunchroom would be a clue that we were no longer satisfied with bologna soup as nourishment. Can you imagine what happened? Can you guess who received credit for the idea?

During Jimmy Carter's term as president of the United States, Alex Haley's *Roots* was presented on television as a miniseries. Teachers assigned the nightly episodes to be analyzed and discussed the next class day. All educational levels watched the programs. At the same time, President Carter had announced the members of his cabinet. A mother in town had taught her first grader the names and positions of each cabinet member. I do not know why she chose to do this, but when I learned about the child's mental feat, I decided to invite the child and her mother to my history class. I thought her ability to name and identify these people would be an inspiration to some of my sluggards. Randomly, I called out the cabinet position; without hesitation, she accurately named each person. When we finished, I was so impressed and so hopeful that she had made an impression on my class that I asked her, "And who are these people who will help President Carter run our government?" Thinking she would reply "His cabinet," can you imagine how I felt when she proudly answered "His slaves"? She had watched all of *Roots*. My class was delighted that my efforts to show them up had not been completely successful.

Each year, the Humanities students went to the Civic Center in Huntsville to see a production staged by the Broadway Theater League. I had always seen the production before taking the students, so I knew that it had an approved rating, but then I made a mistake. In a moment of temporary disarrangement, I made arrangements for seventy Humanities students to have dinner at Twickenham Station, a popular Huntsville restaurant, and to attend *Sugar Babies*, starring Mickey Rooney and Ann Miller. My only excuse for taking the students to see something I had not personally checked out was that I had a picture in my mind of Mickey Rooney as Andy Hardy!

We traveled in two school buses—the boys in coats and ties and the girls in Sunday attire. Practicing table manners taught to the class by a lady from a local jewelry store, the students enjoyed a festive meal. Then happily we went to the Civic Center, took our seats in the theater, and were swiftly caught up in the magic of the surroundings. Have you ever seen *Sugar Babies*? From the opening moment,

I recognized the fact that I had made a dreadful error in judgment—that, in fact, if any one of the seventy souls entrusted to my leadership and care wished to have me removed from my position, this play was all the ammunition they needed. Mickey Rooney played a lewd judge who spoke vulgar phrases as he leered at the actresses whose dresses (or lack thereof) advertised their avocations. The skits were scandalous; the dancing, daring. Limbs were flung about in every sort of pose suggestive of promiscuity. Even Ann Miller left little to the imagination. Honestly, I do not know who registered greater shock—the students or I. They tried not to laugh, but vulgar though they were, some of the skits would have tempted Puritanical souls to a subdued chuckle. Finally, in the darkness, which helped to conceal my embarrassment, I went up and down the rows to tell them I had really goofed, but as we were there, we might as well enjoy it. No one told on me, so I told on myself. My principal hit the ceiling. He began his tirade by sarcastically inquiring if I next planned to take the group to see *The Best Little Whorehouse in Texas*. I didn't.

There were a few situations during my forty years of teaching that left dark bruises on my heart. These situations were caused by disobedience on the part of some students and arrogant pride on my part. I loved all the students involved, and they were well aware of this love. It is my contention that sometimes we make rash statements or even dim threats that we feel constrained to enforce to the hilt, or else, we feel that our authority will be questioned or even challenged. A teacher who truly cares about the students and genuinely enjoys teaching will risk being hurt severely because on the other side of the seesaw are all the joys and pleasures of the teaching profession. Teaching is the most rewarding work. "Work is love made visible," said Khalil Gibran, and I would substitute the word *teaching* for the word *work*.

3.   I learned that people who do not make mistakes are seldom in the arena; they are in the stands, watching and waiting for someone else to make a mistake.

I love to read bumper stickers, signs along the highway, and even printings on T-shirts. Ralph and I saw a wonderful bumper sticker many years ago on the campus of Ole Miss just after the head football coach had been dismissed. The informative sticker read "Will Rogers never met—." Isn't that neat? Once at an antique shop in a rural section of South Alabama, my friend and I were getting out of my car when a battered red pickup truck wheezed to a stop beside us. An emaciated cigarette-smoking bearded elderly male emerged from the truck about the time we saw the bumper sticker attached to his ancient machine. "Immoral Minority" it proudly proclaimed. He certainly looked like the poster boy for this group.

Embarrassing moments punctuated my teaching career. Once, a superintendent of education whom I did not admire and who had warned me once that I was impertinent (can you imagine that?) decided that our high school faculty had become lethargic in our efforts to motivate the students. He arranged for some lady with a talent for motivation and a doctorate to support it to speak to the faculty. That particular day, I had suffered a severe headache. In an attempt to stay at school and complete my duties, I took some little red pills prescribed by my physician. At the end of classes, we had a faculty meeting to hear this lady instruct us in the technique of motivation. I was given the dubious honor of introducing her; therefore, I had to sit on the stage of the Little Theater with her and the superintendent of education. She spoke monotonously. She droned on and on. Would you believe that I dozed off? The combination of headache, end-of-the-day weariness, and little red pills overwhelmed the tips to motivation. My friends on the faculty cleared their throats, coughed, and made other noises designed to attract my attention; but I was slipping away into a delightful stupor when I realized that my body and my chair were no longer compatible. Jerking myself back to reality, I sat there—a mute monument to the visiting professor's lack of motivational skills with me. The superintendent of education considered my actions a personal affront.

One of the many flaws in my character is a short temper. I recognize this fault and try hard to correct it, but I do not always succeed. I do not remember what the catalyst was, but in the principal's office one day, I exploded with the level of a Mount Vesuvius eruption. The driver education instructor was present and witnessed my profane performance. Later that day, we had a faculty meeting that the principal asked me to open with prayer (prayer was permissible in those days). Before I could speak, the driver education instructor suggested to the group that someone else might have a better communication link with the Lord.

On some days, it was quite difficult to whet the appetites of students for events in America's past that shaped the progress of our civilization. Actions that featured violence and calamity held their interests far more than political debates and philosophical discourses. In my history classes, the book was always supplemented by outside reading papers, documents, biographies, autobiographies, etc. The students knew that textbook reading was mandatory, so often, I gave a pop quiz simply to determine who was doing the required reading. One day, I received a strange answer to the simple question "Identify Roger Taney." Instead of answering with any number of positions in which Mr. Taney had served this country, one student whose interest apparently was captured more by photography than by the written word wrote, "The ugly man whose picture is on page 248 in the textbook on the right-hand corner." This site was accurate, but I deemed the answer unworthy of a correct response.

Knowing that I was the focus of the looks of the students (though some only glanced at me as if a smear of knowledge was sufficient to meet their needs), I tried to be as attractive as I could with the resources granted to me. When Dan was about three years old, sun-kissed hair was the rage. How I wished to have my then dark-brown tresses in fashion! The cost was almost prohibitive to a principal/teacher salary schedule, and Ralph was directly opposed to the idea, but I whined and complained about the state of my locks until he finally gave in. With great joy and much anticipation, I went one afternoon after school to a local salon where I received the treatment I had so long desired. I was greatly disappointed with the outcome; I was not the beautiful person the advertisements had proclaimed. Actually, I looked rather strange. As one student would declare, my hair looked like molasses with butter streaked through it. When I arrived home, our dog Bandit tried to bite me as I entered the backyard through the gate; Dan burst into tears, thinking someone had transformed his mommy; and Ralph simply shook his head in a way I knew well how to decipher. School the next day was even worse. The principal—whom I loved and admired but with whom I had fought many battles with—announced over the speaker system that all faculty, staff, and students should be sure to go by my room during the course of the day. The color finally grew off, and I learned a valuable lesson.

The only other time I put color on my hair occurred much later when I was almost totally gray. From Calhoun Community College, I was dispatched to Dothan to participate in a seminar. The sessions began on Friday and concluded the next day. In a weak moment prior to making the trip, I had permitted my friend to put a temporary brown rinse on my hair. So on Friday, I was a brunette. That night, I decided to wash the color out, so when I appeared at the meeting on Saturday morning, I sported my normal gray hair. A pipe-smoking principal from South Alabama was standing on the steps as I approached the building. He hailed me thus: "Mrs. Brett, I don't know what you did last night, but you must have had a hell of a time."

4.   I learned that mistakes can be great lessons. The mistake of the past may be the success of the future.

In my opinion, panty hoses are an abomination conceived by someone with a warped sense of style and humor. In the late autumn one year at Calhoun Community College, my friend who was our division secretary asked me to go with her to the Decatur Mall during lunch. On the way there, I realized that I should have gone to the restroom prior to departure; therefore, while my friend went to do her quick errand, I sought the comfort station. My lower body was clad in panty hose and lined skirt that did not require a slip. I do not understand how the back of my skirt was caught in my panty hose at the waist without my knowing it, but it was. I prissed all the way through the shoe department at Parisian; I never felt a breeze around my bottom. I was totally unaware of my oddity in dress until I heard my friend's agonized cry. When I turned around, she gestured to call my attention to the situation. Somehow, this incident was related in Athens. How do I know? Four weeks later, I spoke to a youth group at church, the title of my talk being "Overcoming Obstacles." When I finished, the pastor asked the group if they had any questions. Would you believe one lad stood and said, "Mrs. Brett, will you tell us about the time your skirt got caught in your panty hose?" The pastor said if he could have caught my expression on camera, the youth might have raised some much-needed cash by selling the pictures.

Many years ago, when drug infestation first threatened our schools, a colleague and I were sent to Calhoun Community College to attend a drug workshop. To my later dismay, the gentleman from the State Department of Education knew me. There were probably fifty teachers in the meeting. Seated directly n front of us was a portly lady (usually gentlemen are portly, but the adjective fits this woman well) whose outfit was accessorized by a belt made of small brass rings—many, many small brass rings. Suddenly she sneezed, her belt broke under the pressure, and those little brass rings flew everywhere. The area around our seats was littered. To this day, I do not know why that incident was so hilarious to me, but I became almost hysterical with suppressed laughter. To try to get control, I thought of death and tragedy, but each time I would almost conquer my mirth, I would see one of those little brass rings lying on the floor, and off I would go again. The gentleman in charge said, "Mrs. Brett, would you like to share the source of your hilarity with the group?" I felt like a third grader being reprimanded for unruly behavior. I declined to share and tried to straighten up.

The Humanities Club at Athens High School each year presented a pageant, which featured the talents of the students. Each did whatever he or she wished in order to showcase his or her special gifts. We did skits patterned after television programs, songs, dances, and orations. The money raised from these pageants was used to finance the educational/fun trips the group took each spring. When I left Athens High School to become the director of the Honors Program at Calhoun Community College, I began doing these pageants with the Honors students, administration, faculty, and staff. We had titles that suggested the theme of each show such as "Putting on the Ritz" or "A Touch of Class." Everyone cooperated when asked to participate, and actually, we had great fun. The Calhoun productions were presented at the Princess Theater in Decatur. The dress rehearsal of the first production was so disastrous that the academic dean—whom I greatly respected and who was doing a piano solo on the program—said to me on the way out of the theater, "I may kill you." This threat so startled me that I determined that I would not meet my demise because of an entertainment faux pas. I spent the next day with different participants as we attempted to fix all that was not good. We did! The performance was superb! We played to a sold-out house; there was not one snafu, and a yearly tradition had its birth. The Monday after the performance, the academic dean called me to his office and said, "What do you want as a bonus for a job well done?"

I replied, "A parking space with my name on it." Alas! I had requested the impossible boon. I never received it.

In his second year of college, one of my five nephews was involved in a bad automobile accident. He apparently went to sleep late one afternoon on his way home. The car turned over; he was not wearing his seat belt and was ejected from his Saab, which was totally consumed by fire. He was taken to Huntsville Hospital with severe injuries. Ralph and I, along with his parents, were there when the ambulance arrived, and I spent the night at the hospital with his mother. On my way home early the next morning, I was harassed by an impatient driver who rode my bumper until he was able to pass. When I realized that he was about to pass, I arranged the fingers on my left hand so that my index finger protruded, and then I positioned my hand in the window. I figured a person as rude as he could appreciate the significance of this first-time gesture for me. He had a look of pure amazement on his face when he saw this gray-haired elderly lady using a contemporary method to convey to him her displeasure at his impatience.

There are times when anonymity is a blessing. One night, I needed to call a friend of mine. Hastily, I dialed her number, and a woman answered. "Margie?" I inquired dubiously because I thought the voice was different from my friend's voice.

"No, this is [false name]."

"I'm sorry. I must have dialed the wrong number," I apologized. Immediately, I dialed what I thought was Margie's number again.

"Hello," a voice said.

I began talking at once. "Margie, I thought I had dialed your number a minute ago, and I got a lady with the weird name of—."

A cold voice responded, "And you have her again."

CHAPTER FIVE

Delicate Feastings and Lofty Undertakings: My Family

Members of my immediate family and my extended family recognized and appreciated the value of an education. My parents always provided what I needed and wanted to attain my educational goals. They never hesitated to furnish the frills and were ever ready to support my endeavors.

May I share with you some anecdotes about my family that will indicate the high regard in which we hold one another and that will show how our diverse qualities have complimented our relationships through good times and bad?

Family support is vital to a teacher's self-confidence. Also, a sense of humor is a must. My sister Mary McCoy—who is now retired but who was a superb physical education teacher in elementary, high school, and college levels—furnished our family with wonderful incidents, which we have enjoyed through the years. Her husband was a high school coach, president of two community colleges that merged, and presently a retiree. Once, when their only child was about three years old, Mary put a dozen eggs on to boil for his Easter basket. She promptly left to play tennis. When she returned, the eggs had boiled dry, the pan was ruined, and little bits of egg were scattered about. The odor was very disagreeable. Her family lived just up the hill from our backyard in the subdivision directly behind us. We were at home, practicing togetherness, when Mary burst through the back door. She was so upset that the three of us ran with her to her kitchen as quickly as possible. We were confronted with a scene from an abstract painting with an accentuated sense of smell. It was inconceivable that twelve eggs could inflict such damage. We cleaned the kitchen, but the smell lingered a great while.

When Mary taught at Calhoun Community College, she enjoyed the distinction of being the only person on campus to have major damage done to her vehicle by a runaway wheelchair occupied by a panic-stricken watch repairman, and she probably still holds the position of being the first disconcerted customer to return a new mixer to Kmart with a cake mixed in it and oil dripping into the batter like chocolate syrup.

When Dan and his best friend were about five years old, Ralph and I were startled by a revelation as we drove home from Sunday school and church. Ralph was driving and I was in the passenger seat and Dan was standing on the back floorboard. As he leaned between us, he said, "Daddy, I'll bet you don't know what me and Whitt [I always wanted to write a story entitled "Me and Dan" or "Me and Whitt"] did in Sunday school today."

"No," Ralph answered, fully knowing that what was about to be revealed probably had little to do with spiritual matters.

"A little girl pulled up her dress, and me and Whitt looked."

Immediately, Ralph began a stern discourse relating to matters of courtesy concerning the actions and apparel of little girls. Then Dan, after a considerable pause, said, "Daddy, I didn't want to look, but Whitt made me."

In that same vein, at the age of three, Dan first saw that wonderfully patriotic poster of Uncle Sam pointing his finger and saying "I want you!" I read it to him, but before I could explain the significance of it, he asked, "Momma, what do he want me fer?"

When the same two lads were high school seniors, they were inducted into the National Honor Society, much to the delight of their parents. Inductees are never told prior to the event, so on the day of the ceremony, there are some surprised students, some disappointed students, and some complacent students who are confident they have made the roster. Dan and Whitt fell deeply into the first classification; they were totally taken aback. At the reception that followed, each inductee was asked to make a remark, and I shall always remember that Dan's remark was "The renegades have broken the ranks."

In November of 1990, our only grandchild, Brock Elizabeth, was born. Anticipating my enjoyment as a grandmother, I retired in August after forty years of teaching. My anticipation of joy has been completely fulfilled as we have had years of sheer pleasure in her company. She talked at a very early age. One day when she was not yet two, she was playing in the den as I sat nearby. Suddenly, she looked over at me and innocently asked, "Lib, have you ruined me?" Then

I knew that—somewhere, somehow—I had been the topic of discussion, which those adorable ears had overheard. To my gratification, one of the first words she spoke was that Southern standby *tacky*. Can you imagine how happy I was to hear that precious thing describe an action with a word that held a place of honor in my vocabulary?

The other grandmother and I shared school transportation duties. One day, when Brock was in kindergarten and I was there to pick her up after school, her splendid teacher related to me privately an incident that had occurred that day. In the opening week of school, the students had been given classroom rules to memorize so they would know what was expected of them and the consequences they would face if they did not live up to these expectations. One day, the teacher was called from the room; she admonished her small charges to behave in her absence according to the rules they had learned. When she returned a short time later, she opened the door to bedlam—students running, playing, yelling, so engrossed in *not* observing the rules of behavior that they failed to notice that she had opened the door. Do you know what Brock was doing? She was standing on top of a work table shouting, "Remember rule 3!" Rule 3 was "Stay in your seat when the teacher is out of the room." Brock was not only out of her seat; she was standing on a tabletop. Some of my friends remarked, when I related this incident to them, that my bossy qualities had emerged in this tiny individual.

In December of 2003, when the infamous Saddam Hussein was captured, my violent streak (my mother sometimes called it a Hitler complex) emerged, and I said in Brock's presence that Hussein should be chopped into little pieces and distributed throughout his land. The very night after I had made this most-unbecoming-to-a-Sunday-school-teacher remark, I saw on his biography on A&E that he had done that exact treatment to some of his victims, the difference being that the body pieces were returned to the families of the victims. Later, Brock voiced what I had said to her father who admonished her for such thinking and asked, "Where did you get such an idea?" Quickly, she indicted me by answering, "From the mouth of your mother!"

Setbacks in the personal lives of teachers will occur—events that one wished the students would not know. Once, I received a speeding ticket on a major Athens thoroughfare late in the afternoon, and I do believe half of my students passed as I was pulled over. Another ticket came in 1997 when my ninety-year-old mother and I were going to a small town in northwest Alabama to pick up several Christmas cakes that an enterprising and talented baker had made for my friends and me. We had carpe diem. December had arrived, and the weather was beginning to herald a glorious Christmas. As we rode along, we watched for hawks sitting on fence posts or in naked trees and chatted about where we would eat lunch. I happened to glance in the rearview mirror where I beheld a heart-stopping sight—a state trooper vehicle with blue lights flashing. Forthwith, I pulled over. The keeper of the law stepped to the window on my side of the car. When I reluctantly lowered it, he said in a gruff tone, "Lady, where are you going? I have had the blue light and siren on for several miles, and you made no move to pull over. I thought I was going to have to radio ahead for a roadblock to stop you."

"I cannot believe that I could not hear that siren. Are you sure it works?" I inquired with all the innocence I could muster.

He returned to his vehicle and sounded the siren—loud and clear it was. I am sure that trooper never engaged in the pleasant hobby of counting hawks, so I did not bother to tell him that my foot must have been pressed harder on the accelerator with each bird we sighted. Instead, I began to extol the wonders of the Christmas cakes we were about to procure. Apparently, he was not interested in gourmet goodies because he handed me an early Christmas present—an eighty-dollar ticket. As he walked away from my Honda, he was shaking his head. It was perhaps the first time he had stopped two Golden Oldies speeding along, looking for hawks, and ignoring blue lights and sirens.

My mother was one of God's unique creatures. She knew not the quality of hypocrisy; she spoke her mind with clarity until her death in January of 2003 at the age of ninety-six. She enjoyed many friends on all levels of society, and she received an average of twenty-five phone calls a day. She enjoyed these calls, though if a call came at an inconvenient time for her, she might display a wee bit of irritation. One day, not long before she died, she told me that she had received so many phone calls that day that she was sure "that damn phone had shortened her days." For a time, she relished one soap opera. She stopped looking at it when, in her words, it became too trashy. She informed me one day that a certain young man who came to visit her was wearing an earring in one ear. With a look of disdain, she said to me, "That means he is a lesbian, you know." Obviously, my mom had little knowledge or real interest in today's sexual patterns.

She was fiercely protective of her three children. In the winter of 2002, Mary and I took Momma to an optometrist in Huntsville. When we were finished there, Mary wanted me to go to a boutique for a short while. Momma opted to remain in the backseat of Mary's Xterra. The temperature had risen, and Mary had taken off her fur vest. When we exited the vehicle, she tossed it across the back of the passenger seat. The windows were slightly tinted, so I suppose the burly bearded man who drove in and parked next to the passenger side of Mary's vehicle failed to see Momma. As he tried to open the front door where the vest was, Momma pulled a toy pistol from her purse and shouted, "You get away from here!" And so he did!

How fortunate I am to have been married to Daniel Ralph Brett for fifty years as of August 14, 2004. We were overjoyed when our only child was born in 1960. I was very indulgent with and tolerant of that bundle of joy. At times, I forgot that the English language contained the word *discipline*. When he grew up and chose his life's partner, Cathy Whitt, we were over the moon because we already loved her. To celebrate the engagement, Ralph and I took them to dinner at a restaurant in Huntsville where we often dined. Soon after we were seated, Ralph excused himself to go to the restroom. He stayed and stayed and stayed. Fearing that some mishap had befallen him, I asked Dan to go check on him. Jubilant with laughter, the two of them returned to our table. In his haste to dress for this happy occasion, Ralph had put his underwear on backward. He could not locate the body part necessary to perform a function related to the urinary tract because the opening was on the wrong side of his body. Later, he remarked that his first thought had been that I had sewed the opening together as a joke, but realizing my lack of skill as a seamstress, he had discarded that notion and accepted the fault as his own. At least, Cathy had a bit of warning about the family she was about to join.

My brother, four years younger than me, had a distinct bearing on my life. An outstanding athlete (Little All-American, Florence State, 1955), he helped me early to develop a love for sports. I am sure that my appreciation for a healthy body was fostered more by Brub than for my love for the ancient Greek culture's philosophy of a sound mind in a healthy body. My love of sports was an asset to me in relating to students who loved the competition of a sports event more than that of a scholars' bowl tournament. Brub and his late wife, Barbara, and their bevy of boys—Bill, Barry, Brett, and Bruce—have been an integral part of my love of life and of education.

In 1983, Ralph and I were elated when Dan and Cathy were married on a snowy December day in the chapel of First United Methodist Church. Cathy has been such a blessing to our group; however, one day she made a remark that greatly amused both of us. Dan had gone deer hunting, and she and Brock (then about two years old) were going with Ralph and me to Panama City, Florida, to visit Ralph's mom. We were discussing the problems associated with old age when Cathy said, "You know, Dan and I were talking about this the other day. I have three sisters to help with my parents, but Dan and I will have you two by ourselves." She did not realize how this remark sounded; and when we laughed, she quickly apologized for sounding so desperate about coping with our future needs. Ralph could not resist saying that we would try to depart the planet before we caused any major calamity; however, we feel confident she would care lovingly for us.

Usually, students do not perform well in required courses in which they have little or no interest. When I was in the ninth grade, a course entitled home economics was required. Cooking classes in this course were enjoyable. Not only did we learn to concoct certain delicacies—we were also allowed to consume them. But sewing and ironing were completely unacceptable to me. The teacher was one of the few I had in all my educational instruction whom I did not admire. In fact, I do believe that I disliked her. Now I recall that she had to endure my bad attitude because I resented having to take the class. If she enjoyed any vice, I am positive that students like me caused overindulgence on some days. When we reached the sewing part of the course, I realized that I really was in trouble. I simply could not unite scraps of material with stitches. (After Ralph and I were married, one morning, he asked me to sew a button on his shirt. Wishing in those early days of our marriage to be a dutiful wife, I sat down with this shirt in my lap and promptly sewed the button on his shirt and my skirt. That ended my days as a married seamstress.) With shame, I now admit how I finally managed to get those pieces of material fastened together—I slipped the whole mess out, took it home, and Momma sewed it for me. Guess what? She made a C! I tried to remember how much I had disliked this required course when students in required courses I taught had indifferent feelings.

Mary's husband, Larry, played football for Bear Bryant at Alabama and was a very successful coach at Athens High School. Of the old-fashioned school, he demanded dedication and discipline from his athletes. When the team had not performed to his standards, they dreaded trotting off the field and into the dressing room. Had a course on "The Art of Throwing Tirades" been offered at the University of Alabama, Coach McCoy could have taught it. He was in the midst of such an exhibition at the half of a game when the Eagles were down by a couple of touchdowns. Suddenly he shouted, "The problem with you is that you have no pride!" whereupon he turned to the blackboard and wrote in big letters: PIRDE.

Years later, a lineman who witnessed this performance related it to me. I laughed, and then I asked, "Did any of you get tickled at this Dan Quayle spelling?"

"Are you crazy?" was his response.

My forty years of teaching ended in August of 1990 because I was about to become a grandmother. I had loved my career in education, but my grandmother genes were taking priority. What happiness! For her tenth birthday, Brock chose a trip to Scotland for her, her parents, and Ralph and me. Ralph and I had been there before and had absolutely loved the beauty of the countryside, the tradition of the old towns, the French cuisine in the local pubs, and most of all, the graciousness of the people, so we were eager to share our experiences with the little family we so adored. We had a splendid time as we traveled in a rented SUV up the western coast, north to Inverness, and down to the eastern coast to Saint Andrews, where we spent the night at a magnificent hotel on the Old Course. Every town and village we visited during our ten days held a special interest as we had talked about everything prior to the trip. We spent one night at Sterling Castle near where Braveheart fought so valiantly.

Dan and Cathy often went to a pub after dinner because they enjoyed the dialogue with the locals. At Sterling, they had a most pleasant encounter with a Scottish couple from a nearby village who were spending the night at Sterling Castle as some celebration. Dan and Cathy excused themselves for a little while to return to our hotel room to tell Brock and us good night. While they were gone, an American couple from Chicago sat with the Scottish couple who told these northerners what a good time they had been having with the couple from Alabama. Imagine Dan and Cathy's amusement when the Scots told them the response of the Chicago couple: "Did you check the color of their necks?"

I cannot write about family support without mentioning a Boston terrier we had for eleven years. He was named Bulleye for the dog called Bullseye in the stage play and movie *Oliver*. Somehow, when we named him, we omitted the *s*. When we got him, he looked like a wee black-and-white rat. He cried so pitifully the first night that I wrapped him in a towel and put him in the bed with Ralph and me. Later, my mom made him a mattress, a quilt, and a pillow; but he still preferred our bed. He made every step I made. When I sat down to grade papers, he was either cuddled against me or in my lap. I lavished such love on him that a child who did not know we had Dan but who had witnessed my love for Bulleye once said to me, "Mrs. Brett, have you ever thought about having a child?" Bulleye did not tolerate company after nine o'clock. He would progress from one guest to the other, take a defiant stand in front of each, and commence to bark. Once, a dinner guest who failed to leave as quickly as Bulleye deemed appropriate was completely taken aback when Bulleye took a flying leap and bit him on the nose. (Ralph and I were taken far aback—we were so embarrassed and apologetic.) Actually, Bulleye sampled a fair section of the Athens populace. He was well known for his cantankerous canine behavior. When we had to have him put to sleep, I had an ache in my heart for many moons.

When my nephew Mike was very young, Ralph and I took him to the Christmas parade. It was bitterly cold, and a group of people huddled in a cluster in front of a bank near the end of the parade. The person dressed as Santa Claus was riding in a sleigh. As he neared our group, he saw Mike hoisted on Ralph's shoulders, and he shouted, "Merry Christmas, Mike!"

I said, "Isn't that sweet, Mike? Santa gave you a special Christmas greeting."

Imagine my frustration when, very audibly, my beloved nephew answered me, "Yes, Santa is a sweet old son of a bitch!"

Locker-room talk taught to the innocent young son of a coach. If you think that I was frustrated, you should have seen the faces of several elderly ladies standing nearby.

When Dan was six years old, we moved into our newly constructed home where we still reside. I stress the fact that the house was new because that truth has a bearing on the situation. At that time, Dan was taking (supposedly) some vitamin tablets, the flavor of which he evidently disliked a great deal. We moved into our new abode in June, and everything was perfect until late autumn arrived and the heating system kicked in. Immediately, we began to smell a faint, not completely unpleasant odor. As winter progressed and the days grew colder and the heat stayed on longer, the smell increased in intensity and became decidedly disagreeable. We examined the house upstairs and downstairs, but we were never able to ascertain the source of the smell, which we had elevated to *odor*. Deciding that the scent faintly resembled that of burning rubber, we called in electricians who examined all the wiring. Nothing was wrong.

Just before Christmas, for some reason that he does not know even now, Ralph lifted the vent cover in the downstairs powder room. There he discovered a mound of orange vitamins that Dan had been depositing since June. Why he slipped them down the vent instead of flushing them down the commode remains a mystery. Ralph's suggestion that we wrap the warm vitamins in Christmas paper and present them to our child was countermanded by a mother's love.

Well, there you have it—why I loved being a teacher. Rarely did I arrive without an eagerness to get to school. I wanted to be a stepping-stone for those whom I taught, and I shall always treasure my memories of being a teacher.

TEACHER-BY-TRADE

I have never climbed Mount Everest, but I have scaled the heights—because I was a teacher.

I have never kissed Brad Pitt, but I have had many thrills—because I was a teacher.

I have never been listed on the Four Hundred roster, but I have been a member of an exclusive set—because I was a teacher.

I have never won a lottery, but I have been very fortunate—because I was a teacher.

I have never traveled around the world in eighty days, but I have explored magnificent minds—because I was a teacher.

I have never sighted a new star, invented a time-saving device, or directed a Broadway play, but I have been very productive—because I was a teacher.

I have never served on a judicial body, but I have used Solomon's wisdom—because I was a teacher.